W9-AJS-720

THE WINE OF GENIUS

SACRE-COEUR ET RUE SAINT-RUSTIQUE

by Maurice Utrillo

THE WINE OF GENIUS

A LIFE OF MAURICE UTRILLO

BY ROBERT COUGHLAN

HARPER & BROTHERS, PUBLISHERS, NEW YORK

THE WINE OF GENIUS, *A Life of Maurice Utrillo*

Copyright, 1950, 1951, by Robert Coughlan

Printed in the United States of America

All rights in this book are reserved. No part of the book may be used or reproduced in any manner whatsoever without written permission except in the case of brief quotations embodied in critical articles and reviews. For information address Harper & Brothers, 49 East 33rd Street, New York 16, N. Y.

FIRST EDITION

I-A

Library of Congress catalog card number: 51-11895

FOR PATRICIA ANN

CONTENTS

	ACKNOWLEDGMENTS	ix
One.	THE MYSTERY	1
Two.	MONTMARTRE AND THE PAINTERS	6
Three.	SUZANNE VALADON	17
Four.	MAURICE—THE EARLY YEARS	31
Five.	THE WHITE PERIOD	39
Six.	FRIENDS AND PROTECTORS	50
Seven.	MODIGLIANI	60
Eight.	SUCCESS AND DESPERATION	72
Nine.	LUCIE PAUWELS'S GREAT AWAKENING	85
Ten.	SUZANNE'S LAST DAYS	93
Eleven.	A NEW LIFE	98
Twelve.	EPILOGUE	109

THE ILLUSTRATIONS WILL BE FOUND IN A SEPARATE SECTION FOLLOWING PAGE 84.

ACKNOWLEDGMENTS

To *Life* Magazine, in which some of the material of this book previously appeared; to Jane Wilson for editorial assistance; and to Vivian Campbell for invaluable help in research and translation.

To the Saidenberg Gallery for permission to reproduce "Sacré-Coeur et Rue St.-Rustique" by Utrillo; to Bernes, Marouteau et Cie, for the family portrait by Valadon, the drawing of Utter by Valadon, the profile of Utrillo by Valadon and the portrait of Gaby by Valadon; to Bernheim Jeune et Cie for the photograph of Utrillo as a student, the drawing of Utrillo at eleven years of age by Valadon, the "Lapin Agile" by Utrillo and the painting of his own arrest by Utrillo; to the Editions du Chêne for "The House of Mimi Pinson" by Utrillo, reproduced from the book *Utrillo* by M. Gauthier; to *Formes et Couleurs* for the photograph of Valadon's studio and the photograph of Valadon taken shortly before her death; to Patricia Collins for the photograph of Lucie and Utrillo; to N. R. Farbman for the photograph of Utrillo in the Lapin Agile; to Dmitri Kessel for the photograph of Utrillo praying.

THE WINE
OF GENIUS

CHAPTER ONE
THE MYSTERY

On December 26, 1883 in a room on the Rue du Poteau in a haphazard neighborhood of Montmartre, an 18-year-old girl called "Suzanne" Valadon gave birth to an illegitimate child. Montmartre then was still almost a suburb of Paris, with gardens and vineyards tucked away among the twisted old streets. But at the top of the hill in the area known as the Butte, where the streets fork off from an open square and interlace the upper slopes, the artists had established themselves in dozens of little courtyard studios. Here the girl had come each day, climbing up the hillside to pose and often staying on into the night to take part in the life of the district. She was beautiful and undisciplined, a gamine of the streets; and somewhere on the Butte, with some man who has never been finally identified, she formed the liaison that resulted in the birth of her child. The baby was named Maurice. For years he had no surname but then was given one, as casually as he had been conceived, by a friend of Suzanne's who offered his own out of sympathy for her. It was duly recorded on the official register of the district: "Maurice Utrillo."

This child, so literally a product of the Montmartre art colony, grew up into a career exactly appropriate to his origin. For forty years he has been one of the important figures of modern art. His paintings hang in every gallery that pretends to cover the modern era and in leading private collections throughout Europe and the Americas. They hang also, in the form of reproductions, in many thousands of Main Street sitting rooms, for Utrillo's work is popular among ordinary people who simply like to look at something pleasant on a wall. Mostly they are scenes of Montmartre streets, squares or vistas. Sometimes they contain no human figures at all, and there rarely are more than a few, usually women, crudely painted, as static as dolls, big-hipped and dressed in the fashion of forty years ago. It is the streets and buildings themselves that interest Utrillo; the physical Montmartre of ancient, stained walls, cafés with colored signs, red-tipped chimney pots, pitched roofs and the living geometry made by the little buildings set like children's blocks on the crooked streets. He paints them with love and respect and devotion, giving them a warmth of color and a dignity which they do not possess in fact. Above all, the pictures have an air of luminous peace, of quiet and strength.

That is an extraordinary thing about them. For Utrillo is a tormented man. In a milieu where neuroticism is almost a necessary card of admission, and where lunacy has so often accompanied genius that there is a tendency to confuse the two, he very early established his own legend. He was a drunkard at the age of thirteen. By the time he was eighteen he was a dipsomaniac and was ready to be sent off to an institution for the first of a series of "cures." The greater part of his life has been spent in the murky world of the alcoholic; and the record, like his life, is blurred. Now and then a scene looms into the foreground. . . .

1913, Montmartre, in the small hotel of his friend M. Gay. Utrillo has asked Gay to lock him in a back room on an upper story with his paints and canvases and not to let him out. All goes well until nightfall; then Utrillo begins to call from the room, to knock loudly, to beat and kick on the door. Gay holds to his promise. Utrillo shouts and then screams, careening around the room, upsetting paints, canvases, furniture. A crowd gathers outside. At last Utrillo breaks open the windows, jumps, lands unhurt and runs off into the night to search for a drink.

1921, a street in Paris. A drunken man lurches out of a urinoir. His clothing is dirty and disarrayed, his hair is matted and he is unshaven. He waves a half-empty bottle in one hand and shouts insults at the passers-by. It is Utrillo. The police come and take him away.

1924, No. 12. Rue Cortot, Montmartre, at the studio where Utrillo lives with his mother, grandmother and stepfather. He has been gone for two nights and a day, and Suzanne, fearing that he has had an accident, has spent the night looking for him. On the morning of the second day the police bring him. He is sober but half dead. His face is raw, his scalp is laid open and there is a bloody cloth around his head. The police say that they picked him up from a gutter and took him to jail, and there in his cell he beat his head against the walls and tried to kill himself.

Yet, to be set against such scenes as these, there are the pictures, more than two thousand of them, mostly of Montmartre, almost all with the soft and nearly classic serenity that no one has quite been able to imitate. Usually art reflects the personality of the artist; but there is no easy connection between Utrillo and his work. Nor is it enough to ask why he paints in a certain spirit, for the method of his art is equally surprising. Living in the time and place where modern art was born, among those who created it, he is perhaps the least "modern" of the important living painters. It is a mystery, the solution of which would perhaps furnish the key to the larger mystery of Utrillo's personality.

If no final solution may be ventured, there are at any rate certain pieces of evidence and certain clues. They involve some understanding of his era—if only to know the influences that ordinarily might have been expected to make him a different artist from the one he became. They involve, in an even more important way, the personality and career of his mother, Suzanne Valadon, who undoubtedly was the greatest influence in his life. And they involve the character of Montmartre itself, the obsessive subject of nearly all his paintings.

This, then, is not so much a "life" of Utrillo as an attempt to illuminate the grand hallucination that has been his life.

CHAPTER TWO

MONTMARTRE AND THE PAINTERS

"Ah, Montmartre, with its provincial corners and its Bohemian ways, how many stories could be written on this section of Paris—so independent and original in itself. It is unfortunate that the unhappy state that brought me here has not passed. I would be so at ease near you, sitting in my room, composing a motif of a street of white-washed houses or all the other things . . . !"

—FROM A LETTER WRITTEN BY UTRILLO TO HIS FRIEND CÉSAR GAY, FROM THE ASYLUM AT VILLEJUIF IN 1916

In the garden of the Church of Saint Peter, where Suzanne Valadon in the piety of her old age used to attend Mass, and from where she was buried, there still remain stones from a Roman temple. Montmartre is very old; perhaps as old as Paris, for just as the islands of the Seine gave a natural protection so did the steep Butte, rising more than three hundred feet above the plain. Its name comes from the legendary martyrdom of three Christian missionaries, one of whom, Saint Denis, is said to have taken his severed head and walked with it until he found a kind woman who would give him burial. Montmartre's recorded history began in 1096, with the founding of a monastery, which in the next century became a Benedictine Abbey, which in turn became a part of the Church of Saint Peter. More abbeys, monasteries, and convents followed, until by the thirteenth century the Butte was known as the "holy hill." There were thirty-nine windmills, all church property, which helped support the religionists by grinding grain from the surrounding countryside. The slopes were covered with vineyards except on the southern side, where gypsum quarries produced the rock from which is derived "plaster of Paris."

Gradually, over the next few hundred years, the character of Montmartre was reversed. As a convenient stop on the road to Paris and a sanctuary for fugitives who for various reasons might have to escape from the city, it developed a thriving tavern trade; and in time the taverns outnumbered the monasteries. By the seventeenth century Montmartre was notorious as the seat of every kind of vice and crime, which went on despite remarkably strict police regulations. Prostitution, along with gambling and drunkenness, flourished behind such pious signs as *L'Image Sainte-Anne* and *Aux Armes de Madame l'Abbesse.* Murders were commonplace: in one week there were ten. At last the village's reputation grew so fearsome that only criminals or the most adventurous citizens visited there, with the result that most of the taverns and brothels were forced to close. Deprived of income from sin as well as religion, Montmartre settled back to live on its own resources: the windmills, the gypsum mines, the gardens and vineyards, and such goods as local artisans produced. By the middle of the nineteenth century it was respectable and rather somnolent, a country village despite its nearness to Paris. Parisians now came for the view, or to spend Sunday afternoons sipping the potent local wine and perhaps dancing at the Moulin de la Galette, an old mill that had been converted into a middle-class pleasure resort.

It was in the late 1870's, during Suzanne Valadon's childhood, that a third transformation began. The artists and writers, sculptors and musicians who frequented the Latin Quarter, far off on the other side of the Seine, now began one of those spontaneous migrations that so often shift the artistic center of a city from one spot to another. By 1880 the trend was well established; and it would continue until the village had become the center of Parisian creative life and, accordingly, the fountainhead of those influences that still shape modern art in nearly all its forms. Night life and gaiety arrived along with the artists. A number of *cabarets artistiques* sprang up, and there were many café concerts, music halls, dance halls, and resorts of all varieties. This was the lively, vivid, and often dissolute Montmartre that fascinated Toulouse-Lautrec and inspired so many of his best and most famous pictures. But unlike the earlier time, amusement never became Montmartre's chief industry, much as Lautrec's pictures may leave that implication. The village bloomed only at night. In the day, it seemed essentially unchanged: peaceful and rather provincial, a picturesque tangle of smoky plastered houses and crooked streets and hidden gardens, all set along the hillside and atop the commanding Butte in the unordered growth of two thousand years.

Among the *cabarets artistiques* perhaps the best known, at least among the painters, was the modest Lapin Agile. Thanks to the sentiment of Aristide Bruant, the great *chansonnier* who was such a friend of Lautrec's and who bought it to save it from the apartment builders who were destroying many of the old Montmartre landmarks, it survives even now almost unchanged. It is a low cottage, looking very much like a village farmhouse, set back from the street and shrouded in trees. The original structure was built for Henri IV as a shooting box: a convenient resting place after the chase in the nearby forest, and convenient also to the house of Henri's mistress, Gabrielle d'Estrées, who lived near the Church of

Saint Peter. To this "long room," which was to become the actual cabaret later on, had been added a kitchen and several smaller rooms, so that the box became a small but complete house. At various times it served as a home and a tavern, but seems to have acquired its name during one interval when it was the studio of the caricaturist André Gill. For some reason lost to history he painted a large white rabbit above the door, and this unexpected "lapin à Gill" naturally became a landmark. The critic and historian R. H. Wilenski tells how the youthful Rimbaud, arriving in Paris to try his fortunes, and carrying a note of introduction from Gill's pupil Forain, came to the house and, finding Gill away, went to sleep on the sofa. Gill returned in a few hours, discovered his uninvited guest, gave him ten francs and sent him packing—one of the first but not the last of the rebuffs the poet was to suffer. From "Le lapin à Gill," in due time, came the pun, "Le Lapin Agile" (the agile rabbit). After Gill's tenancy the house again became a tavern, known as Les Assassins, and was frequented both by apaches and artists, with the latter finally making it their own. Under the regime of the famous Frédé and Berthe as host and cook respectively the name became officially "Le Lapin Agile," and so it has remained.

If modern art was, in a sense, born on Montmartre, it was in the same degree nourished at Le Lapin Agile. Frédé (Frédérick Gerard), the jovial proprietor, was a true addict of painting. He had started his own career as a draughtsman but had found that his real talent was that of *bon vivant* and host and had drifted into the cabaret business. He played the guitar and sang in a strong baritone, preferring to do so while sitting astride a wine barrel, leading his customers in the choruses. Artists, as he knew from his own experience, often had no money; in that event they ate and drank on credit, which most often they liquidated with the gift of a picture. To raise the cash to keep this happy ménage in being Frédé each morning hitched his pet donkey, Lolo, to a cart piled with pictures and fresh fish, and accompanying himself on the guitar, would shout his mixed wares through the Montmartre streets. Some of the artists' offerings he could not, or would not, sell; and thus the walls of Le Lapin Agile became crowded with works of art, including a large harlequin painting by Picasso and an enormous wax crucifixion by Wasselet. Naturally, this sympathetic atmosphere attracted a clientele. The names now read almost like roll call of the great moderns: Picasso, Vlaminck, Van Dongen, Modigliani, Derain, Braque, Poulbot, Marie Laurencin, Dufy, and their friends in the allied arts, Max Jacob, Pierre MacOrlan, Guillaume Apollinaire, Francis Carco, André Warnod, among many others.

The Lapin Agile was in the peculiar tradition of French art, where the café has served somewhat the same function as the coffee house in eighteenth century English letters—a casual forum where ideas were exchanged and subjected to informal criticism and winnowed to their core of merit, if any. The process still goes on: now the locale is in St. Germain de Prés, at such places as the Flore and the Deux Magots, the post-War II counterparts of the famous Dôme and Rotonde in Montparnasse where Cubism and the other extremist experiments were nurtured in the years before and after World War I. The very beginnings of modern art go back to a café, the Guerbois, on Avenue de Clichy, at the foot of Montmartre. They coincided almost exactly with the birth of Suzanne Valadon.

Certain aspects of the art called "modern" can be traced back to the Byzantines, to the Egyptians, and, indeed, to the cave dwellers; which proves only that aesthetic truths have a way of becoming lost and of having periodically to be rediscovered. But the first big landmark in the development of the matrix of ideas and techniques that define modern painting came in 1863, when the Emperor Napoleon III created the Salon des Refusés as a catch-all for the paintings that had been refused by the academic Salon des Beaux Arts. The sensation of this rump exhibit was a picture by Edouard Manet called "The Bath" (afterward retitled "Lunch on the Grass"), a large composition showing two young men and a young woman, the latter naked, lolling in a glade beside a stream. The Empress, when she saw it, was so shocked that she looked the other way and passed by while the Emperor said sternly, "It offends modesty" and largely on its account made this the last as well as the first Salon des Refusés. The general opinion was that Manet was a vulgar sensationalist.

The reason for the uproar was not that the woman was undressed. The female form, more or less undraped, was an accepted fixture of academic art. Heretofore, however, it had been shown in the allegorical references and formal postures of classical art, or else in the remote and essentially unreal subjects of the romantic art which, at the time of the exhibition, was the dominant school. The trouble was that Manet used no excuse for his picture: here were real people in a real setting, shown with the informal candor that would have been recorded by that new invention, the camera. With "The Bath," modern Realism in art was launched. Its credo was that life in every aspect, the ugly as well as the beautiful, the immediate and plebeian present as well as past or faraway events, is material for the artist, whose duty it is to capture moments of existence. From this, it followed that Realist pictures often appeared somewhat unfinished: for to capture the moment, the artist had to work fast; or at any rate, whether he actually did so or (as often happened) finished a picture at leisure in his studio, the appearance of haste and spontaneity added an extra flavor of reality to his product. His pictures were or pretended to be quick impressions. And from this came the term "Impressionism," which was to be another rallying call for artists in the latter half of the nineteenth century. Working fast and generally out-of-doors, the Impressionists naturally became acutely aware of the changing values of light at different hours of the day. With some of them, in due course, it became an end in itself to capture these changes: one finds the same scene painted again and again in different lights by the same artist. This led to a general brightening of the palette and to carefully worked-out theories of color, particularly to the use of "divided color"—the juxtaposition of small dabs of harmonizing colors which, when viewed from a few feet away, blended into a single and "living" color.

These ideas did not spring into being full-blown from Manet's brow in 1863. He and such predecessors as Courbet had done other, though less provocative, realistic pictures before; and Impressionism, as a fully defined and intellectualized approach to painting, did not emerge for some years afterward. To be a Realist, moreover, was not necessarily to be an Impressionist. Nevertheless, the two doctrines, which often are thought of as separate, were in fact so closely related that it is convenient to speak of this first period of modern art as Realist-Impressionist. It became a "movement" as the result of the admiration felt for Manet's pictures by four young friends named Renoir, Monet, Sisley, and Bazille. They had visited the Salon, and a showing of Manet's at a private gallery, and were so entranced by this approach to painting that they jointly quit the classes of their academic master, a man named Gleyre, and resolved to follow suit. Thereafter, beginning in 1865, they formed the nucleus of a group that met frequently in Montmartre at the Guerbois, Manet's favorite cafe. In the next five years, until the Franco-Prussian War, this was the Senate and G.H.Q. of the Realist-Impressionist forces. Degas, Cézanne, Pissarro, and several other artists became habitués, as did the great pioneer of literary realism, Emile Zola, and a number of other writers and critics.

They made small headway. Indeed, it was not until 1873, with the Franco-Prussian War over and the postwar disruptions finished, that the group felt strong enough to launch Impressionism officially with a joint exhibition. It was received by the public with amusement, and by the critics with disdain. They persevered with other exhibitions, however, with gradually more success, until by 1880 they were established with many of the important collectors and dealers, and had at least as many critics for them as against them.

It was that year that Suzanne Valadon began her career as a model. Thus she arrived on a scene in flux. Among the artists who were swarming into Montmartre were Classicists, Romanticists, and Realist-Impressionists along with individualists and opportunists. They brought along their disputations, and their periphery of critics, models, hostesses, dealers, entertainers, suppliers, sycophants, and dilettanti. They brought their Bohemianism, their intensity of feeling, and their eccentricities. They brought life and excitement.

Montmartre in the early 1880's would have stirred the imagination of any ordinary girl. And Suzanne Valadon was far from ordinary.

CHAPTER THREE
SUZANNE VALADON

My mother, a saintly woman whom I bless and venerate as one would a Goddess, a sublime creature of goodness and rightness, of Charity, Intelligence, of Courage and of Devotion, a choice woman, perhaps the greatest light in painting of this century and in the world, the noble woman has always brought me up in the most strict precepts of morality, truth and Duty.

Alas, that I didn't follow her sincere advice and was dragged through the road of Vice and became a repugnant drunkard, the object for derision and public disrepute.

Alas, a hundred times alas . . . that my creator will forgive me. . . .

FROM AN AUTOBIOGRAPHY WRITTEN BY MAURICE UTRILLO DURING 1914-18. THE MANUSCRIPT IS NOW OWNED BY PAUL PETRIDES

She was born Marie-Clémentine Valadon on September 23, 1865 in the village of Bessines near Limoges, 270 miles southwest of Paris. When her son was born and she was required to give her own birth date on the certificate, she put it down as 1867. She maintained the deception all her life, so successfully that the museum catalogues and other biographical sources report it as fact. The birth records at Bessines show otherwise. Why, at the tender age of eighteen, especially in view of the circumstances, she should have preferred to be thought younger is perhaps a precocious indication of the sense of drama that was to distinguish her throughout her career.

She was an illegitimate child. Her mother, Madeleine Valadon, was a peasant girl. The father's name is unrecorded, and all that is known of him is that he worked in a flour mill and was killed a year or two after her birth when a millstone fell on him. What kept her parents from marrying is not known. In any case, while Marie-Clémentine was still a small baby her mother, presumably disgraced in the village and unable to stay there, brought her in a basket to Paris and settled on the Boulevard Rochechouart in Montmartre, where she became a charwoman. It was a hard and poverty-ridden life, with money for only the barest essentials and sometimes not for them. As a tiny girl, Marie-Clémentine was sent often to beg stale bread and leftovers from the restaurants. She had a few years of schooling at a nearby convent and thus learned to read and write and do simple arithmetic; but that was the end of her formal education, and from the age of about nine she worked. She sewed, sold vegetables in the open central market, cleaned houses; when she was old enough she became a baby nurse. There was no consistency in her life. In 1870, when she was five, the Franco-Prussian War came, and with it the French defeat, the German occupation of Paris, the Commune, the second—and greatly destructive—siege of Paris under Thiers and General MacMahon, the subsequent White Terror. The Third Republic was not established in real peace and stability until 1878, when she was thirteen. The surrounding turmoil only made it harder for Madeleine to make a living, and she had little time for her daughter. Often she worked at night, scrubbing offices after the hours of closing. As a result of all these circumstances, as well as of an inquisitive and adventurous disposition, Marie-Clémentine became far wiser than she should have been for her years.

Her unattended wanderings naturally had taken her to the Place Pigalle, which had become the center of Montmartre night life, and to the Cirque Molier, a little permanent circus established there. She was in her adolescence, but her figure was well formed, and in spite of the rigors of her childhood she was strong and lithe. She made friends with the leader of the acrobatic troupe, and persuaded him to train her. Soon she was a member of the act, and ordinarily might have passed the next years happily in the life of the circus. Only six months later, however, she slipped from a trapeze and had a fall that nearly killed her and left her with a permanently injured back. Luckily there was no paralysis or outward deformity, and in most ways she was able to lead a normal life afterward; but there could be no question of returning to the troupe.

One day in 1880, when she was well enough to work again and was wondering what to do, a neighbor girl called Clelia, who made her living as a model in the artists' colony on the Butte Montmartre, offered to introduce her in that trade. Marie-Clémentine had a strikingly attractive face, blue eyes, a prematurely ripe and appealing figure, and a saucy personality; her success was rapid.

Probably the first artist to employ her more than casually was Pierre Puvis de Chavannes. Although only middle-aged he was almost a relic from the past, when painting, under the influence of the Empire, was classic and artists, following the examples of the great David and Ingres, made a point of respectability. Puvis de Chavannes was primarily a muralist, and he painted in the style called "neo-classic." He liked to cover great areas of wall or canvas with allegorical scenes, which he populated with Grecian nudes and reclining—or sometimes flying or floating—nymphlike women in diaphanous drapery. A typical product is his "Sacred Grove," containing fifteen figures for most of which, both male and female, Marie-Clémentine posed. She worked for him at various times over a period of seven years. His studio was some distance away at Neuilly; and often, at the end of the day, he would walk with her back as far as the Place Pigalle. His attitude toward her was at first fatherly, but she made it difficult for any man to maintain that feeling for long. It is almost certain that she soon had an affair with him.

Another of her earliest employers was Auguste Renoir, who was one of the first of the subsequently famous painters to live on Montmartre, and whom she met at the Cabaret des Assassins long before it became the Lapin Agile. Her hair, which was later to turn almost black, was then a deep red-blond—Rodin, the sculptor, described it as the color of cognac—and along with her agile body and gay nature made her a complement to Renoir's favorite model, Gabrielle. He used her often as a subject for his nudes, posing her in the garden of his house on the rue de la Barre, where the tall lilac bushes shielded her from the eyes of the pilgrims who trooped by on their way to the unfinished Basilica of Sacré-Cœur. She modeled also for the famous companion pictures, the "Country Dance" and the "City Dance" —but whether for one or both, or one and only part of the other, is impossible to determine. She always declared she was the model for both. But Madame Renoir had become jealous of her, and to prevent a domestic crisis the painter used his wife for some of the posing and convinced her, at any rate, that she had supplied the inspiration for the girl in the "Country Dance."

Within a year or two she had established herself as one of the most popular models on the Butte. She worked hard; and after work she plunged with uninhibited zest into the excitements afforded by Montmartre life. Madeleine scolded and warned, but night after night there was some inducement—a studio party, a gathering at some café, or, when some friend could afford the price, dancing and entertainment at one of the gaudy cabarets that were springing up here and there on the Montmartre slopes. She was often at the *cabarets artistiques*, which catered particularly to the artists and models and their friends in other creative fields. It was at one of these, the newly opened Chat Noir, that there occurred a meeting that was to have an important effect on her life.

This place was on the Boulevard Rochechouart, near the room where Madeleine and she had lived when they first arrived in Paris. The proprietor, Rodolphe Salis, a former painter, was a flamboyant charlatan who liked to dress in odd costumes and affect the speech and manners of the era of Louis XIII. He furnished his cabaret in the same style, with armor, carved woods, antique weapons, hunting trophies, and a huge fireplace dominating what he called the "great hall." He was a shrewd and persuasive showman, and he not only attracted a talented clientele but managed that they supplied their own entertainment. The poets recited their newest poems, the musicians gave concerts, the actors declaimed, the playwrights wrote scripts for shadow plays, the journalists published a weekly magazine to which the artists contributed drawings—while Salis presided bombastically and made money. The group included such diverse names as Anatole France, George Auriol, Guy de Maupassant, Paul Verlaine, Sarah Bernhardt, André Gill, and Jean Louis Forain, as well as many lesser personalities and, of course, the camp followers that such an assemblage would attract. Among the latter was a young man named Boissy, who made his living as an actuary at an insurance company but who was by temperament a dilettante and Bohemian. He had hoped to be a painter but had no talent, and consequently gratified his impulses by painting occasionally on Sundays and by frequenting the artists' cafés and cabarets at night. The son of an alcoholic father and a mother who committed suicide to escape her unhappy marriage, Boissy was himself a chronic alcoholic and libertine. But evidently he had attractive qualities. Marie-Clémentine met him at the Chat Noir one night; and soon she had formed a liaison with him that was to continue for several years, until he died of his compounded vices.

Boissy probably was the father of the child who became Maurice Utrillo. In the legend that has grown up around Utrillo a number of men, including Puvis de Chavannes, Renoir and Degas, have been suggested for the honor. Undoubtedly there were various possibilities; and Marie-Clémentine, in her fanciful way, seems deliberately to have kept the matter a mystery, while tacitly encouraging the idea that the man was one of the famous artists. Even her son grew up unsure of his paternity. Perhaps, indeed, Marie-Clémentine was not sure. But among her intimates, at any rate, it was always assumed that Boissy was the father, not only of Maurice but of another son who was born later but died in infancy. There seemed to be no disposition on either side to marry, and certainly there was no urging from Madeleine. On the contrary, whenever Boissy ventured to call for Marie-Clémentine at home, Madeleine would upbraid him and turn him away from the door.

The birth of a child seems to have affected Marie-Clémentine at the time as merely one among many incidents that added variety to her life. The greatest change was that Madeleine stayed at home to mind the baby and take in sewing, as she was able to do now because Marie-Clémentine made almost enough from modeling to support the household. They moved from the rue du Poteau to the rue Tourlaque, near the Church of Saint Peter, in the very heart of the Butte. Marie-Clémentine went on as before, now eighteen and with an absorbing new interest that had nothing to do with parenthood.

One morning in 1883, the year of the "City Dance" and the "Country Dance," she had been late in coming to Renoir's studio. In spite of her late nights she was ordinarily punctual about work. Renoir waited, began to worry, and finally decided to walk to her home nearby to investigate. He found her, completely absorbed, standing with crayons and pastels in front of a nearly finished self-portrait. She was embarrassed and said nothing, but stood so that her body cut off his view of the picture. Renoir, smiling, said, "You, too?" But then he took a closer look at the portrait and his amusement gave way to surprise. "And you hide it?" he exclaimed. The picture was good—amazingly good considering that she never had had a drawing lesson. It hangs now in the Valadon-Utrillo room of the Museum of Modern Art in Paris.

Encouraged by Renoir she did more drawings, not daring, however, really to take herself seriously as an artist. She was in a good position to learn by imitation, and she paid close attention as her employers went about their business. But she took none of them as a master. She did not copy, and her technique owed no more to Renoir than to de Chavannes, and no more to him than to a dozen others. It developed but remained her own: hard, clear, exact lines, in simple but forceful compositions, carefully placed and harmoniously balanced. She showed the pictures to her good friends; among them, in due course, Toulouse-Lautrec, whose encouragement was perhaps, directly and indirectly, the decisive factor in changing her career from that of model to artist.

This strange genius has been described by Gerstle Mack as

> a hideous little creature with a huge head, heavy eyebrows, an enormous fleshy nose, immensely thick lips that were very red and moist, and a short but bushy black beard that concealed his chin and partly covered the sides of his ruddy face. His ugliness was grotesque. His eyes, sparkling and intelligent, compensated to some extent for the unloveliness of the other features. But even they were far from perfect: decidedly myopic, they were disfigured by the thick lenses of a pince-nez attached to a black cord. His torso was ponderous, stocky, and ungainly. To complete the unprepossessing picture his body was shockingly ill-proportioned. From the waist up he was of average size, but his legs were so abnormally short that his total height did not exceed four feet six inches, and so weak that he could walk only with the aid of a diminutive cane. They were the legs of a child feebly supporting the heavy body of a man. . . .

He had come to Paris in 1882 to study painting and enrolled under the academic master, Bonnat, in the latter's studio on the western slope of Montmartre, up from the Place Pigalle and behind the site where the Moulin Rouge was soon to be built. Attracted by the district, he took an apartment and a studio, and from about 1884 until his death made Montmartre his home.

Naturally he met Marie-Clémentine. They were nearly the same age, and soon she became both his model and friend—one of the few male friends with whom it was not assumed that she had an affair. He loved the Montmartrian atmosphere of gaiety, license, and sincere work which so exactly matched his own temperament; and it is not surprising that he was attracted to Marie-Clémentine, who typified this same spirit. She was often at his house for parties, where some of the best talk in Paris took place, and on occasion some of the most imaginative orgies. For a time she lived in the same house on the rue Tourlaque, near the cemetery of St. Vincent, where he had his studio.

At the time of their early friendship Toulouse-Lautrec had no reputation as a painter, but his money, his social position (he was heir to the noble house of Toulouse-Lautrec Monfa) and to some degree his evident talent gave him a special status on Montmartre. His attitude toward her was that of affectionate patron. She brought him her drawings, which he liked so well that he hung them on his walls. He amused himself by asking his visitors to identify the artist; and they, assuming that it must be someone of importance, often guessed the name of one or another of the established painters. His interest became so proprietary that he changed her name. "Marie-Clémentine," he told her, was too banal a name for anyone who wanted to become a great artist. "Suzanne" was more stylish, and also suited her personality.

"Suzanne Valadon" she became. She is listed thus in museum catalogues and in all the records of her era. The change in identity was complete; and she will be called by her assumed name hereafter in these pages.

Toulouse-Lautrec's advice and encouragement meant a good deal to her, naturally; but coming from a contemporary who was himself only a beginner, they were subject to some discount. Perhaps his most valuable contribution to her development was to send her to his friend Degas, who was then established as one of the leading spirits of the Realist-Impressionist group and, indeed, as one of the most respected painters in France. He was Toulouse-Lautrec's special hero. The younger man, upon first arriving in Montmartre, had selected a studio in the same building and across the courtyard from Degas's studio, and thus had managed to meet him and finally to create a friendship. One of Degas's firmest opinions, he knew, was that a "natural talent" in painting or drawing could not, by itself, produce anything of real merit—that long study and practice are necessary before anyone so gifted could produce a durable work of art. Toulouse-Lautrec thought that Suzanne's work disproved this theory, and accordingly he arranged an introduction.

With her portfolio and a letter from Toulouse-Lautrec, she went off one day to the great man's house. Zoë, his faithful and formidable housekeeper, took the letter inside, and returned in a few minutes to say that

Degas would see her. She entered with considerable apprehension, for except among his intimates Degas had a chilling personality: austere, querulous and moody, the reflection in part of a lifelong hypochondria. She put down the portfolio and nervously took out each drawing in turn, while Degas watched and said nothing. The disturbing silence continued while she went on like an automaton. Then, at the end, Degas smiled and said, "You are one of us." She had absorbed some of Toulouse-Lautrec's vast admiration for Degas. Now the Master had spoken, and she could believe that she was really an artist.

The episode marked the beginning of a long friendship. Probably Suzanne was the only woman, besides his American pupil and protégé Mary Cassatt, whom Degas ever wholeheartedly liked during his adult life; for it was ironically true that this painter, who was able to distill the essence of femininity in his ballet pictures and some of his nudes, and who devoted much of his career to painting the female figure, had an abiding distrust and antipathy toward women. For Suzanne he obviously felt real affection. He coached her and encouraged her (although she usually failed to take his advice) and called her his "wild Maria." His regard is shown in surviving letters: "I send you my best and beg of you again, if you are well, not to abandon drawing. You have a genius for it. . . ." And again, "From time to time, I look at your drawings hanging in my living room. And I always tell myself, that deviltress Maria has a genius for drawing, why doesn't she show me anything more?" It has been supposed—and Suzanne did nothing to discourage the belief—that they had a physical attachment. Perhaps so; but a firmer foundation for their relationship was Suzanne's gift for bringing cheer to Degas's perpetually morose outlook. She was gay and friendly and disconcertingly honest, and she lived life as fully as he rejected it. Moreover, semi-recluse though he was, Degas liked gossip; and she, who was everywhere on Montmartre, entertained him with her lively accounts of the loves, tragedies, and scandals that went on outside his door.

Her friendship with him, with Toulouse-Lautrec and all the others, her newly discovered talent as an artist, the increasing diversions of Montmartre life—all this was a great deal more interesting to Suzanne than her accidental motherhood.

CHAPTER FOUR

MAURICE—THE EARLY YEARS

Meantime Maurice grew into a strange little boy. He had a thin but pretty face, with blue eyes and dark straight hair, and a rather delicate body, small for his age. He was tense and terribly shy, and even in games among other children held to himself, quieter than the others, reserved and uncertain. Now and again Suzanne would take him for a walk, perhaps down the rue Caulaincourt past the Saint Vincent cemetery to the Boulevard de Clichy, the scene of so many of her evenings; or again, to the studios of the artists. He remembered later having gone to the houses of Degas and Toulouse-Lautrec, and at the age of five having met Renoir at the Lapin Agile. Sometimes Suzanne would pet and caress him with all the lavishness of her nature. But these were crumbs and fragments: for the most part she forgot about him, or seemed to, and left him in the custody of Grandmother Madeleine, whose attitude toward him mingled her resentment against Boissy, her disapproval and occasional antagonism toward her daughter, and a maternal protectiveness for the diffident child who was, after all, her own grandson.

At five he started at the communal school near the Basilica of Sacré-Cœur, but he did poorly. Madeleine, who was illiterate, enlisted another elderly woman, a friend named Mariani, to teach him to read, and he proved apt enough so that by the time he was ten he had read one of Emile Zola's books. But meantime his shyness had become morbid. He rarely smiled and seemed never to laugh. He had fits of overwhelming and futile temper. When he was opposed, he would shriek, "I'll break everything," or "I'll jump out of the window and kill myself." Madeleine was distraught and puzzled. "He's a sweet darling," she would say, "but I wonder what he has in his blood. He frightens me sometimes."

When he was seven, Suzanne formed a liaison with Paul Mousis, a well-to-do lawyer who worked for an importing company but who had many friends among the Montmartre groups. He was an attractive and kindly man; Suzanne always remembered him afterward with affection and respect. But among the qualities that drew her to him was his bourgeois propriety, which survived despite his Bohemian associations; and it was this same factor, particularly his pride in his family name, that made the existence of small Maurice a complication when the time came that he asked Suzanne to marry him. He was kind to the boy, even fond of him; but he made it clear that he could not allow him to bear his name. Maurice had been registered at birth as the child of an unknown father—whether because Boissy refused to recognize him, or because Suzanne really was not sure of the paternity, is not clear. In any case he had no name, and with Mousis's refusal he was unlikely to have one. Suzanne, in whom a sturdy peasant respect for such amenities underlay an otherwise free spirit, worried about this so audibly that it became the concern of the whole Butte.

There is a legend that one day at a café she was telling her trouble to a young and unknown artist named Miguel Utrillo, who sympathized and then asked, "But who *is* the father?" "I can't decide whether it was Degas or Renoir, that's the difficulty," Suzanne supposedly replied. "I would be proud to sign my name to the work of either artist," Miguel Utrillo said. "Call him a Utrillo."

Whatever merits this may have as an anecdote, the facts are different. Miguel Utrillo was a journalist, essayist and architect. Born in Barcelona in 1863 of an aristocratic family, he came to Paris in his early twenties and soon became a well-known figure on Montmartre, where for a time he even had a room at the Moulin de la Galette, and later at 57 Boulevard de Clichy. He worked mainly as a journalist, but his good spirits and wide talents made him popular among the artists and the various others who coalesced in the society of Montmartre. He was a habitué of the Chat Noir and knew everyone there, and was a particularly good friend of both Erik Satie, the composer, and Paul Mousis. Since the first had already had an affair with Suzanne, and the second was having one, he naturally felt an interest in her problems. When the difficulty about Maurice's name came up he solved it with a friendly, light-hearted gesture: he volunteered to give the boy his own. It was a good name on every score, and Suzanne delightedly accepted it. On April 8, 1891, she and Miguel went to the town hall on the rue Drouot where he formally adopted the child, who thereupon became Maurice Utrillo.

There was only one dissenter to this happy solution —Maurice himself. Obstinately and tearfully he clung to the name by which he had been known, Maurice Valadon, and no amount of explanation could make him give up this symbolic but intimate connection with his mother. It was not merely a childish rebellion. Eleven years later, when he began to paint, he signed his work "Maurice Valadon." Later he conceded an initial, and signed "M. U. Valadon," and finally, after other variations—but not until 1910, when he was twenty-seven—settled on "Maurice Utrillo, V.," the signature used on nearly all of his subsequent work.

Mousis's talk of marriage finally matured some five years later in an actual wedding; but meantime, with unaccustomed constancy, Suzanne remained his mistress.

They lived together quite openly, and Mousis explained that it was only the objections of his family that prevented a legal ceremony. In 1893, when Maurice was ten, they decided to spend the months of good weather in the country, in a house on the edge of the little suburb of Pierrefitte. Maurice and Madeleine were established there as year-round residents, and Maurice went to the village school. And at this age he began to drink.

Madeleine, with faith in the tonic properties of wine, had given him heavier draughts of watered wine than most French children ordinarily receive. The house at Pierrefitte was well stocked with wines and liquors, and Maurice had chances to experiment. Too, Mousis was generous with him: he had an allowance, and the café keepers of the village were amused when, instead of asking for an ice or a pastry, he ordered wine. Once, when he was on his way home from school, he was given a lift by some plasterers, who stopped on the way at a café for a drink and jokingly asked him if he would join in. When he did so they were so entertained that they gave him enough to make him thoroughly drunk. He staggered home to Madeleine violently sick; and she, horrified, gave him a long scolding which only made him determined to drink as much the next time and keep it down. Madeleine found it more and more impossible to deal with him. She hid the wine and liquor. But he would threaten, "Give me the bottle or I'll run away and never come back," and usually she gave in. Mousis, whether through tact or indifference, did little to try to control him. Suzanne could always make him behave, but she and Mousis lived in Paris in the winter and she was often absent from Pierrefitte even in the good months, for her career was blossoming in the most promising fashion.

In Maurice's eleventh year she submitted five drawings to the Nationale, an important annual exhibition, and was elated to have all of them accepted. The same year she did her first engravings in Degas's studio, under his guidance, and the following year she worked out a dozen engravings on zinc, using his press. Ambroise Vollard, the dealer who had sponsored so many well-known artists, liked one of them ("Two Young Girls Drying Themselves") and had her pull a hundred copies for sale. The next year she started a painting, "Grandmother and the Little Rosalie," which turned out to be one of her greatest successes. Concurrently she was enjoying her role of consort to a wealthy man. Mousis had a gift for money-making. Very soon he was able to build a substantial house at Montmagny, another village near Pierrefitte. Suzanne kept a hind in the garden and rode back and forth to Paris, where she maintained a studio, in a carriage drawn by a mule and accompanied by two huge wolfhounds. She carried her full part in the gaudy and exhilarating life of gay-nineties Paris. She entertained, developed an appreciation for fine wines and cuisine, knew everyone, and dabbled in such side lines as furniture designing.

Meantime Maurice, his tuition paid by Mousis and equipped with a liberal allowance, had been enrolled at the College Rollin, a preparatory school on the Place d'Anvers in Montmartre, to which he commuted each day by train from Montmagny. He was a bad student except in mathematics, for which he showed a considerable flair. On the corner opposite the Rollin campus was (and is) the Café des Oiseaux, an old establishment replete with marble, oak, and bonhomie, and this was a natural target for Maurice during his free periods. He was still very shy; but he had money, and he formed a few drinking friendships. Soon he had graduated from wine to cognac, and from that to absinthe. If the Oiseaux hesitated to give him as much of it as he wanted and could pay for, there were many other cafés on his route to the Gare du Nord. He became an addict, not merely of alcohol but of this singularly powerful and destructive form of it.

Mousis, seeing that life at the college was doing him little good and much harm, finally withdrew his support and told him to go to work. He found a job with a mercantile house run by an Englishman, where he wrapped parcels, delivered goods, and did other menial service for a tiny salary. A bit later Mousis got him a job with the Crédit Lyonnais, where he used his mathematical talent by adding huge columns of figures all day long. He wore his first bowler hat, which pleased him, and his addition was faultless; but he continued to drink as much as he could afford and his behavior was uncertain. One day, in a rage, he broke an umbrella over his superior's head; and that was the end of that job. He tried a few others, which lasted only briefly, and then gave up and went back to live with Madeleine at Montmagny. He drank everything he could find or steal.

At last, unmistakable signs of disintegration came. He began to have alcoholic tantrums in which he would shout crazily and scream with obscure fury. Mousis insisted to Suzanne that he be committed to the nearby asylum of Saint Anne. He was then eighteen.

CHAPTER FIVE
THE WHITE PERIOD

Within only two months he was back home again, cured—so the asylum officials said—and looking healthier than he had in years. But it was agreed that it was too soon yet for him to take another job, so he stayed at Montmagny to continue his convalescence. There was little to do: he used his time reading, roaming the fields, walking in the village, where at first he passed the cafés and wine shops in apparent unconcern, and then began to stop in for only a drink or two—and very soon was again an alcoholic. Suzanne remonstrated with him, but this was the one thing in which he would no longer obey her. Finally she remembered the advice of a Dr. Ettinger, a friend who had bought some of the furniture she designed and who had said that some manual therapy, such as carpentry or painting, might have a good effect in distracting his mind from the craving for drink. She persuaded him to try painting.

He took it up to please her, and without enthusiasm. She prepared the canvases for him and he used her own favorite palette of two chrome yellows, a vermilion, Turkey red and zinc white. At first he painted the views he could see from the house windows, but then, growing more interested in the effects he was finding, he moved outdoors and endured the curious and sometimes ribald attentions of the village. His health and state of mind improved slowly. Finally, after two years, he was well enough so that Suzanne felt he should have a chance to live in Paris among the artists.

He was established on the Butte at 2 rue Cortot, only a few paces from the Lapin Agile and a short walk from the Place du Tertre. Across the way was a vineyard, one of the few (and now, today, the last) remaining on Montmartre. Off to the left was the towering white hulk of Sacré-Cœur; ahead, over the rise, was the Moulin de la Galette; below on one side were the roofs of the rue du Poteau, where he was born; that other street led to the elementary school where he had gone every day in his high-laced shoes, dark suit, cape and muffler and hard little black hat. Thus, at twenty, he found himself again among the scenes of his earliest remembrances. Each street and building had some connection with his childhood, and every landmark carried some memory of his mother. In one of those buildings, in a studio or hotel or the back room of some café—he never knew where—he had been conceived.

He began to paint Montmartre.

This was a time of rising excitement among the artists.

Many years before, in 1886, Van Gogh had spent some months in the district, studying at the Cormon atelier along with Toulouse-Lautrec, doing a few scenes of the Montmartre vineyards and gardens, and even attempting a café mural or two for which he was paid in trade. His strangeness and what seemed to be his artistic crudities left him ignored. Toulouse-Lautrec was kind to him, and even carried on a correspondence with him afterward; and Suzanne, who did not like his work but had a sympathetic heart, once rose to the occasion, when he showed a canvas to some of the artists and was met with silence, by yelling at them, "Cows!" He soon left for Arles and was forgotten on the Butte, where his death in 1890 caused hardly a ripple. But then his reputation began to grow. In 1901 there was a retrospective show of his works. It was like an explosion. The younger artists, who had been only dimly aware of him, found in his vivid colors, his distortion of line and form, and his violently expressive use of brush and paint an answer to Impressionism, which by then had become so respectable as to be academic, and so refined as to verge on the insipid. Led by Matisse, a group consisting principally of Derain, Rouault, Vlaminck, Dufy, Friesz, and (briefly) Braque banded together under the name of *Fauves* ("wild beasts," in honor of a critic who called them that) and began to torture color and form in a way that then seemed demented.

Other influences also were abroad. Cézanne, who

had left the Impressionist group early to work out his own special and powerful métier, had at last gained some real recognition with a large exhibition at Vollard's in 1895. His influence grew during the next few years, and at last he was recognized as a great artist in 1904 (when he was sixty-five, two years before his death) with a special exhibition at the Salon d'Automne. Gauguin, too, had left a mark of sorts. Returning from Tahiti in 1893, and temporarily prosperous due to an inheritance from an uncle, he took a studio which he decorated with shells, boomerangs, painted hatchets, and other South Seas trophies, including a lively monkey who ran free and a Javanese girl named Anna, his mistress and hostess. He dressed in a vivid costume of blue coat with pearl buttons, yellow trousers, green hat, and wooden shoes. He went back to Tahiti in 1895, poor again and with syphilis contracted from a Montparnasse prostitute, but sent pictures to his dealer. At his death in 1903 he was fairly well-known and even, among a few artists and collectors, admired.

Besides these great men of the older generation, there soon appeared a young one who was to have an influence perhaps greater than any of theirs. Pablo Picasso had arrived at Montmartre in 1900, at the age of nineteen. He returned twice to Spain but then, in 1904, came back to stay. He took quarters on the Butte at the rue Ravignan, in a big, sprawling house of eccentric design known as the Bateau-Lavoir because of its fancied resemblance to the washing barges in the Seine where poor women did their laundry. In its other studios, and nearby, were Braque, Dufy, Friesz, Derain, Van Dongen, and others of the young artists. They caroused together, borrowed and learned from each other, argued and painted and experimented together; and from them and their circle came the movements and isms and artistic pranks which gave modern art a velocity that is spending itself only now, nearly fifty years later.

All of this meant little to Maurice, however. His morbid temperament kept him from seeking friends and made him a poor companion. He was only dimly aware of the artistic currents of his own time, and lived creatively instead in his mother's generation. What he knew of technique in these early years he learned from her; and his masters in matters of style were the Impressionists Pissarro and Sisley, whose pictures at the Durand-Ruel gallery he used to study often. Sisley especially attracted Maurice, the reason, perhaps, being that he had died only recently, in 1899, and his reputation and the value of his paintings had mounted rather spectacularly. In any case, Sisley for a time was almost an obsession with him. His early Montmartre scenes, like those at Montmagny, are all unmistakably Impressionist; but although they were derivative and for the most part crude, and lacked any of the technical tricks of the Impressionists, they already showed a sense of color and design and a peculiar intensity of conception that indicated an emerging talent. If he knew little about theory, there was yet, in his favor as an artist, the deep compulsion to express something, although it was not a thing that he could consciously define.

He worked fast, usually finishing a painting in one burst of energy, and during his first year on Montmartre did about 150 canvases. It was a remarkable production, especially considering that he had begun to drink heavily again. In a matter of months he was out of control, and by mid-1904 it was necessary to take him back to Montmagny. He improved there, and continued to paint. One day in his rambles he met André Utter, a plumber's son, a youth three years younger than he, also an artist, who had left the swirl of Montmartre for a rest in the country air. Utter, who was to be perhaps his first close friend, recalled later: "Already he had that familiar look of a mountebank Hamlet, with his emaciated face and his disheveled hair. He gesticulated as he walked, talking loudly, clearly subject to some congenital nervous excitement which could not be appeased. But even so, he painted." Utter painted with him, then and later, and having his own share of perversities found him an acceptable companion when, after some months, he was allowed to return to Montmartre. Utter was a roué and semialcoholic and shared in the Montmartre fad of dope-taking. Ether was the popular drug, some preferring it to alcohol, but cocaine, hashish, and the various opium derivatives also were widely used. André Warnod remembers a New Year's Eve party where hashish was served and Utter was there "dancing with his yellow hair sticking up like flames." Maurice used drugs little or not at all, and in the "autobiography" noted earlier took a moral stand against "ether-mania" and told of the terrible effects it had on a young boy he knew; alcohol, by comparison, he said, was almost harmless. Through Utter, a bit later, he met the fantastic Italian, Amedeo Modigliani, who was then in his early twenties. The three young artists were often together and pooled their money and appetites in scores of alcoholic escapades. Maurice entered a period of chronic but not acute alcoholism, in which his days typically began with abstinence and good resolutions and ended in drunkenness or coma.

When he was sober he was tractable enough—very shy, with an air of perpetual anxiety, but unassuming and even rather sweet in disposition. And up to a point, alcohol was a useful crutch: he could laugh and make jokes and talk easily with people. Then, at a certain stage, he became unpredictable. He was attracted to the Lapin Agile and went there night after night; but sometimes, sitting among the gay and noisy crew of artists and models, he might begin to stare around the room and then suddenly to yell and break glasses and bottles. He was capable of worse violence. For a while he nourished a phobia against pregnant women, and when he saw them in the street he would chase them and pull their hair and try to kick them in the stomach. He could be set into a rage or a black silence by an apparent trifle: when, for instance, someone addressed him as "Monsieur Utrillo," the name he still hated. He wanted to be called "Monsieur Maurice," or, among his friends, "Maumau." To many of the ordinary citizens of Montmartre he was, derisively, "the painter." The men sometimes amused themselves, when he came reeling into a café asking for credit, by buying him a glass of wine and then surreptitiously knocking tobacco ash into the glass. The boys of the district would trip him or, finding him stone drunk in the gutter, would strip him to his underwear and hide his clothing.

He painted. Sometimes he would go down to the quays of the Seine or into the streets and byways of Paris. He was at Montmagny often, to see Suzanne and Madeleine and dry out from some prolonged alcoholic bout. His pictures are an almost daily record of his whereabouts. But for the most part he stayed on the Butte and painted, again and again, the street scenes of Montmartre. He experimented with all sorts of materials, even burlap and sticks; and gradually he began to work out a style that was distinctively his own. It still owed something to the Impressionists and perhaps, in his heavy use of pigment, to the *Fauves*. Yet it was unlike either school. It had stability, an architectural firmness, a direct and yet highly personal conception. Most astonishing, it had serenity. His skies were often dark—they have been called "tragic skies"—but they filled the air with luminescence. His streets, deserted except for a few crudely indicated figures, were eternal streets. The colors were warm: Montmartre, thus seen, was mellow and wise and tranquil.

Now and then he could sell a picture, or more often trade it for wine, food, and fresh supplies. In 1905 a former baker named Clovis Sagot, sometimes known as Sagot-the-Madman, began to buy a few for as much as five francs each (the franc was then twenty cents) and ship them off to Switzerland, where he doubled his money. Louis Libaude, dealer and critic, a former horse auctioneer who has been described as having "the air of a card sharper in a hearse," saw some of them at Sagot's gallery in 1909, when Maurice's style had finally formed, and also began to buy. That same year Manzana Pissarro, son of the Impressionist, encountered Maurice under an awning where both had gone to escape a rainstorm. Maurice had a portfolio of paintings under his arm; Pissarro looked at some of them and made a date to come to the studio the next day to see others. He found Maurice standing dirty and unshaven and half-drunk in front of his easel, with a partly eaten sour red herring sticking from his pocket—to increase his thirst, he explained. Pissarro bought ten pictures for fifty francs each, and Maurice stayed drunk until he had got rid of all the money. A few months later a certain Macène, an amateur artist and small collector, bought two landscapes, paying one hundred francs each. That year Maurice submitted four landscapes to the Salon d'Automne, and three were accepted. His elation crashed when his application to enroll for study at the Ecole des Beaux Arts was rejected. Many years later he would remember, when asked to sum up his life, "that was one of the saddest things for me."

In 1910, drunk and brave, he took an armload of paintings to the important Galerie Druet, where M. Druet, regarding them and him with equal distaste, showed him the door. In a fury, he stood outside in the street and tried to hawk them to passers-by for any price they would bring. Francis Jourdain, the critic, was there that day, and saw something in the paintings that escaped M. Druet. Impressed and curious, he went to Libaude's gallery to see more of them, and later he brought Paul Gallimard, Octave Mirbeau and Elie Faure, well-known respectively as publisher, novelist and critic. All three bought paintings. The prices were small—only fifty francs or so—but the prestige of the buyers was important. Word spread on the Butte that Maurice had to be taken seriously as a painter.

He was then at the peak of his "white period," so called because of his lavish use of zinc white (sometimes mixed with real plaster) in an attempt to capture the look of the white stone of Sacré-Cœur and the various off-whites of the plaster that covered so many of the Montmartre buildings. He was twenty-seven. M. Druet

and the others who rejected him would, in later years, have reason to be regretful, for these "white period" paintings are the finest (and most valuable) of his whole life.

CHAPTER SIX
FRIENDS AND PROTECTORS

Suzanne was becoming bored. She had by now achieved some reputation as an artist, mostly with engravings and drypoint etchings, had painted a few oils, and was experimenting with pastels and even with sculpture. But her career was moving more slowly than she desired, and she felt, without knowing how, that she was capable of a more ambitious production. Moreover she was tired of Mousis. He was not a demanding husband, but he and the paraphernalia of conventional marriage took time. She knew that her beauty was going. She had begun to drink a good deal, and the eroding effects of alcohol, the secret affairs she carried on, and age itself had begun to show in her face. And she was worried, when she found time to consider the matter, about what was to become of Maurice. She was used by now to having the police call her at all hours at her studio or in the country. She knew that he had real, possibly great, talent, and she knew that no one could go on living as he lived without a complete smash-up. She felt uneasy and generally dissatisfied.

Through Maurice she had met Utter at Montmagny, and she had seen him casually from time to time in Paris. Edmond Heuzé, a minor artist of the period, supplied to critic André Warnod a glimpse of her as she then appeared: "One spring morning André Utter and I were on the rue Cortot, laboriously painting a landscape, when we suddenly saw a young, small, and thin girl advancing upon us with two big dogs on a leash. She had astonishingly clear eyes, black hair, done very simply, and seemed more to be dancing than walking. She was amazon and fairy at the same time." One day a few years later, in 1909, when Utter was again painting on the rue Cortot, Suzanne spied him from the window of her studio and asked him to come up. Then and there they became better acquainted. Soon she had formed a steady liaison with him. After two years, in 1911, she left Mousis for good and, along with Madeleine, went to live with Utter in the studio he then shared with Maurice at 5 Impasse de Guelma. A few months later the four of them moved to a large studio at 12 rue Cortot, where the previous tenant, Emile Bernard, had written over the door: "Those who do not believe in God, Raphael, and Titian may not enter"; and there they settled.

According to their individual natures, each member could find benefits in this arrangement. Madeleine, who was now in her eighties and approaching senility, had the important things, a home and her family. Utter had Suzanne, for whom he felt a powerful sexual attraction.

Suzanne, free of all convention, could indulge her fanciful nature to the limit. Moreover, although Utter was not and never would become a successful painter, he had taken part in many of the artistic movements of the time and was well-versed in theory and technique, and could guide her out of the cul-de-sac in which she felt she had arrived. Soon she put aside her experiments and devoted herself to oils—sound advice on Utter's part, for it was in that medium that she went on to make an important name for herself. As for Maurice, he not only had his adored mother in the place he loved best, Montmartre, but also had his friend Utter as his *de facto* stepfather.

Somehow the logic of the situation misfired. Maurice drank and drank and drank, and by the spring of 1912 was in a sanitarium at Sannois, on the outskirts of Paris.

The pattern was set and, with variations, it would repeat itself grotesquely over the next decade. Maurice was soon released—"cured" again—and he and Utter and Suzanne celebrated by spending the latter part of the summer in Brittany. He was homesick there for Montmartre, and did only a few melancholy paintings. In 1913 Libaude, who by then had put him on a small monthly retainer, gave him a one-man show; he and Utter and Suzanne spent the summer in Corsica; and afterward he went again for a few months to Saint Anne's. In 1914 Utter was drafted for the army and in a fit of sentiment Suzanne, (having by then divorced

Mousis,) married him before he left for the front. Maurice, of course, was rejected, to his great discouragement. He hated the Germans, but could find no other way to attack them than by painting the bombed cathedral at Rheims. In 1915 Madeleine died at the age of eighty-five, puzzled to the last as to the strange life in which, through some inexplicable accident, she had found herself immersed. Maurice by then was in another institution, this time an asylum for the really insane, where he slept in a barred cell and where the other inmates, when they could, snatched his tubes of paint and ate them, thinking they were colored creams. He was released after eight months and went back to Montmartre. Within a year he was in a hospital; then, the next year, in the home of a doctor who thought he could cure him if he had him under close observation. He left, but later in the same year committed himself voluntarily to a sanitarium at Picpus. He soon changed his mind and escaped, spent a few months in Montmartre, was returned to Picpus, and again escaped. The doctors did not insist that he come back provided Suzanne hired a keeper for him, and so Pierre, a burly but amiable and pious man from the sanitarium, was added to the ménage, which by this time again included Utter, back from the war. Maurice improved, and after a year Pierre was dismissed. The next year he was put under observation in a mental hospital and then taken to another institution for alcoholics.

It was 1921. He had had eight commitments in a little less than ten years.

During this time he was not—except perhaps briefly—clinically insane. His behavior was strange and he always drank too much and was wholly irresponsible when drunk, but neither eccentricity nor alcoholism was a stigma on the Butte, so he was always welcomed back. Those garbled years, in fact, supplied some of the happiest human relationships of his life.

Chief among them, of course, was his companionship with his mother. She kept the studio at 12 rue Cortot, and enlivened it with her irrepressible spirit. Living was difficult during the war, but she always managed somehow to find food and wine enough not only for the family needs but to entertain. If twenty guests turned up at a party, a sheet pulled off her bed and spread in the middle of the studio floor made a picnic cloth. She and Maurice painted together, and lunched and dined, when they had the money, at various little *bistros* on the Butte. She was proud of his work, and as her pride developed so did her feeling of responsibility. She told everyone that he mustn't be given money or drink, and with signs of real devotion she scoured the alleyways and gutters for him when he failed to appear at the studio, and nursed him through the aftermath of his debauches. Still, as always, she had her own life. The Weill gallery gave her a one-man show in 1915; and although it was a commercial failure, she was pleased by the comments of the critics. She was busy with her painting, with little trips here and there, with an active social life. Toulouse-Lautrec and Puvis de Chavannes both were dead, and Renoir had moved to the Côte d'Azur. Of the great friends and protectors of her youth, only Degas remained, now so embittered and neurasthenic that she rarely saw him. But to take the place of these old friends there were many new ones, who at various times included Georges and Nora Kars, Derain, Vlaminck, and others of the rising generation of artists. When the mood took her she went off to visit them; and in 1917 she stayed for a while at Belleville-sur-Saône, where Utter was stationed with the 22nd Infantry. At such times, if they came during Maurice's intervals of freedom, she left him in charge of M. Gay and his wife.

César Gay was one of his most patient protectors in those days, and it was not strange that he was a former police sergeant. Maurice understandably had been on bad terms with the police during his early years, but the passage of time had bred mutual understanding. The police stopped mistreating him, and he learned always to go along with them peacefully. Once he even painted a picture of himself being led away. He kept a supply of paints and materials on hand at the station house, and the police, many of whom had become amateur artists themselves after long association with the inhabitants of Montmartre, established the rule that he could not be released until he had done a picture or two for their collection. At last the chief had so many Utrillos that he used their backs for scratch pads.

Sergeant Gay had retired and opened a little café called the Casse-Croûte on the rue Paul-Féval, where Maurice began to go to drink and listen to the neighborhood gossip and then, as he formed a deeper attachment for the place, to paint and live during the times his mother was away. Gay rented him a small upstairs room and he painted some of his best pictures there, often at night. He had so far grown away from Impressionism that he preferred artificial light to sunlight and he was so shy that he painted from postcards and memory rather than brave a street audience. He was often a trial to Gay. Once when he was refused more wine he stole Mme. Gay's eau de cologne and drank it. Sometimes, at his own request, Gay would lock him in his room with food and painting materials and refuse to let him out until he had finished a picture, although many times Maurice would beat on the door and howl for help. Twice he broke free by leaping from his window: once in 1913, as already described, and again in 1918, when he had escaped from the home of a Dr. Vicq at Aulnay-sous-Bois and taken refuge at the Casse-Croûte. Gay made him sign a pledge, "I swear to stay, without going out, until the end of September. Utrillo V." Until the end of September meant three weeks. Utrillo's resolution lasted only a few days: he jumped from the window, came back later drunk and noisy, and awoke the next day deeply remorseful for having troubled his friend.

Gay hung his pictures on the walls of the café, from where a few were sold and immediately replaced with new ones. He trusted him when he could not pay his five francs a day, treated him as if he were a member of the household, and tried generally to be a fatherly influence. It was at the Casse-Croûte in 1915, between asylums, that Maurice wrote the scraps about himself that he called his autobiography, which he dedicated to Gay with an epilogue of praise for his qualities as a friend. Gay said later, "I reasoned with him, made him understand that he shouldn't drink too much and he would listen to me very nicely. For each canvas he finished I gave him, naturally, his quart of red wine and tried to prevent him from drinking it in one gulp." Gay liked to watch him work, and as a result became so interested that he tried some paintings of his own. Later on, when Maurice's work began to sell for good prices, Gay asked him if he would mind signing his name to a few of them. Maurice repaid his old friend's kindness by doing so, and Gay readily disposed of them. One turned up only a few years ago when Paul Petrides, Utrillo's most recent dealer, received a call from a dealer-friend who asked him to hurry over and look at a peculiar Utrillo he had just bought. Petrides saw instantly that it was not genuine; but when he examined the signature he realized that it, at least, was authentic.

Thoroughly puzzled, he borrowed the painting and took it to Utrillo, who told him the story.

Around the corner from the Casse-Croûte was La Belle Gabrielle, a café named for the mistress of Henri IV and owned by an openhearted woman some twenty years Maurice's senior, called Marie Vizier. She had a warm personality and a tolerant view of life, and her place ran a close second to Gay's as his favorite retreat. He painted a tricolor above the door and Montmartre scenes on the walls. Once he did a picture of the little street, showing a small boy writing on the wall of a building opposite, "Across the street are the best memories of my life." Another time, in an excess of good feeling, he decided to decorate the bathroom while Marie was out for the afternoon. He did murals on the walls, with flowers, birds, and pleasant outdoor scenes. She returned in the dark, went to use the room, and emerged to find her best dress covered with paint. The murals are among his lost works, for Marie, outraged, immediately scrubbed them all off with gasoline. Like Gay, she watched over him. Francis Carco, the critic who was such a fixture at the Lapin Agile and who has chronicled many of the sights and personalities of Montmartre, gives a typical episode:

> "No, Maumau, it's finished," Marie Vizier would say. "Your mother told me to look after you." Then would come the big scene which happened regularly inside the shop. . . . Utrillo couldn't understand.

"What? My mother?" He would mutter, "Why do you bring my mother into it?" And, passing his hand over his face, he added, after having consulted himself, "If you refuse to serve me, you'll never get another one of my paintings!"

"Go cave in!" returned Marie. "And as for your paintings, as you say, or better still, your blobs, for all they're worth—I'll throw you outdoors with them into the street. Do you understand? And you're a real disgrace," she would add—this woman who was always the first to spring to his defense when anyone else started to talk about him.

Among his great contemporaries—the "Picasso gang" at the Bateau Lavoir, the mavericks like Pascin and Soutine, the beginning surrealists like Chagall—Utrillo was known, accepted, and even respected, both as a painter and as an ultimate manifestation of the Bohemianism they all admired. Later on, Picasso was to evaluate him as "one of the greatest French painters" of that time, and Soutine would call him (in 1942) "the greatest painter living today." But he was not especially liked—his personality was too difficult—and he formed a really warm association with only one of them, Amedeo Modigliani. This, indeed, was one of the strangest and surely one of the most tormented friendships in history, and deserves special notice here.

CHAPTER SEVEN
MODIGLIANI

Modigliani was in almost every way Utrillo's opposite. Immensely handsome, he charmed and conquered scores of women. (Utrillo seems to have had only a desultory interest in sex, whether because his instinct was sublimated into indirect outlets, or because of a naturally weak sexual appetite.) Assertive and gregarious, he avoided solitude with as much effort as Utrillo usually sought it. Loquacious and eloquent, he liked to recite Dante and Rimbaud by the page, and he could dominate an argument or discussion with an unfailing glibness. He was wellborn, a descendent on his mother's side of the philosopher Spinoza and on his father's of a bourgeois family that had made money in mining and forestry. He was born in Leghorn on July 12, 1884, and thus was only six months younger than Utrillo. By then his father's fortunes had taken a bad turn from which they never recovered, so that when, at the age of fourteen, he made up his mind to become an artist, it was not easy to find money for lessons. He managed to study in Venice and Florence, however, and in 1906, at the age of twenty-two, realized his dream of coming to Paris. People who remember him as he then was have described him as a well-mannered, gay but temperate young man, marked equally by ambition and naïveté. Filled with the legend of La Bohème, he dressed in a brown velvet-corduroy suit, a bright red flowing scarf, and a broad-brimmed black hat, a costume he never forsook although he soon learned that the real artists preferred dungarees. Within a few months he had established himself on the Butte in a little studio, and with his good looks and Italianate charm he soon was well acquainted.

A remarkable transformation then began. Ordinarily, alcoholism is a disease that needs some time to develop; but Modigliani, perhaps in his zeal to be accepted by the hard drinkers of the Butte, arrived at that state within only a year. Chianti and Beaujolais gave way to absinthe and cognac. It was not long also before he was initiated into the popular vice of hashish, which may have contributed to his unique style of painting. Charles Douglas, one of his biographers (*Artist Quarter*), quoting André Utter as his informant, says that "one night, at an alcohol and hashish orgy chez Pigeard . . . Modigliani suddenly gave a yell and, grabbing paper and pencil, began to draw feverishly, shouting that he had found 'the Way.' When he had finished he triumphantly produced a study of a woman's head and the swan neck for which he has become famous."

Through Utter he met Utrillo, and in spite of profound differences in temperament they became fast friends. This was a source of some astonishment to the Montmartrois, to whom Utrillo was a comic and pathetic figure whose only claim to attention was his capacity for drink; while Modigliani, in those early days, seemed blessed with all the social assets. It was a strange sight to see him, handsome and rather dandified, supporting the drunken scarecrow figure of Utrillo as they left a café. But soon it became a matter of mutual support. Modigliani developed an appetite for drink that could be compared only with Utrillo's; and, compounding this with addiction to dope and an unlimited appetite for women, left the most lurid mark of any of the strange ones of the School of Paris.

André Warnod tells of a party at his own studio in 1908:

> Modigliani stood by the door, and as each person entered, he gave them a hashish pill. The drug put everyone, already very drunk from alcohol, in paroxysms of frenzy. About the middle of the night they got the idea to set fire to an enormous tub of punch. The rum didn't burn, so someone added some kerosene from the lamp. The fire sprang to the streamers which were decorating the studio. Pretty soon, everything seemed to be in flames but no one paid any attention. The best part of that affair was that the damage was very slight. The fire burned up a couple of hangings.

One of the first of Modigliani's numerous mistresses was one Elvira, a demimondaine he had met in one of the Montmartre cafés. He disliked working with professional models and instead used his friends as subjects; the portrait titled "Elvira" is one of his best. A Madame Gabrielle, an old friend of Elvira's, told Charles Douglas about a memorable scene she happened to witness:

"I was coming home one night with friends—oh, it was quite early, about one—and there was a lovely full moon. As we came into the Place Jean-Baptiste-Clement from the Place Ravingnan, we heard a piano going full blast, playing a Spanish scherzo, and a woman's voice, wild and hoarse. We stopped to look. Outside that shed Modigliani had (a carpenter's shop found for him by Utter), to one side, there was a bit of garden, about the size of a handkerchief. Well, a woman in a kimono, nude to the waist, with her hair down, was dancing madly, and opposite to her was Modigliani, in trousers only, capering about like a lunatic and yelling like a demon. Every moment he would turn his head and scream: 'You pig-headed calf! You pig son of Madonna!' at a lighted window in that big house at the back, in the rue Norvine, where lived some kind of Treasury fellow. As we stood laughing he dropped down his trousers . . . and started to caper around her.

"Oh," Madame Gabrielle interrupted herself, evidently affected by the memory, "but he was beautiful there in the moonlight, like a faun, and we all said what a shame it was that he drank like that. Then the woman dropped her kimono and the two danced nude. And then a gang of brutes who were passing started shouting and yelling, and he picked her up. She threw her head back at that moment and I recognized her. As they disappeared into the shed, I screamed,

'Vira! Elvira!' . . . Oh, but they were beautiful, those two, but quite mad with *that*, of course."

Modigliani's paintings and sculpture—in these early years, he was primarily a sculptor—did not sell, and his allowance from his family was not enough to support his appetite for debauch. He picked up money here and there as he could, mainly by doing quick sketches and portraits for a few cents each at the sidewalk cafés. Often he was without working materials. The new apartments that were then beginning to change the face of Montmartre, and to which the artists vigorously objected, were in a sense a godsend for him, for he was able to steal stones and timbers on which to carve. As the years passed with little or no recognition he became embittered, and this mounting disappointment led him to even greater excesses. He grew quarrelsome and troublesome and eventually was disliked even by most of the artists, whose extreme tolerance he managed to wear thin. Among the few people (except for his succession of mistresses) who bore him any lasting affection were Utter, Valadon and Utrillo. Suzanne was attracted to his beauty, liked his work and accepted his violent and sybaritic behavior as a normal manifestation of talent. He told her that she was the only woman who could understand him, because of all the troubles she had had with Maurice; and, in fact, she was one of the few who had any success at calming him when he was in one of his manic moods. Maurice himself, suffering from the same lack of recognition and the same compulsion to drink, naturally felt an affinity for him, and sought him out as a companion who could be counted on never to censure him or to be the first to suggest going home. After about 1910, however, their meetings became increasingly haphazard, for Modigliani began to spend a good deal of time away from the Butte, most often in Montparnasse.

Montparnasse and the adjacent Latin Quarter, several miles away on the other side of the Seine, had been the earlier locus of artistic life, and even after the migration in the 1870's and '80's to Montmartre had remained the favorite of many writers and poets. Now, with Montmartre becoming a tourist attraction, and with its lower slopes a night-club district and the Butte itself changing under the hands of the builders, an ebb tide set in, and Montparnasse freshened with life as Montmartre declined. Modigliani was one of the first to go; and, although he often returned to the Butte, gradually he identified himself with Montparnasse and the life there and eventually made the district his home. The movement across the river took on something of an official nature in 1912, when Picasso left, soon followed by the group of which he was the acknowledged leader. As life on the Butte had seemed to radiate from the Lapin Agile, the center of conversation and the meeting place of Montparnasse became the Café de la Rotonde, on the boulevard du Montparnasse, then a much more modest and intimate place than the large establishment that has taken its name and location. Here, during the next few years, there gathered a clientele exceptional not only for its diverse talents but its mixture of nationalities. Foujita, the Japanese painter; Van Dongen, the Dutchman; Soutine, the Lithuanian; Zborowski, the Polish poet; Picasso, the Spaniard; mixed with Aicha, the Negress model; Modigliani, the Italian; the many French, of course; Pascin, the Spanish-Italian Jew born in Bulgaria; Augustus John, the Englishman; the Americans and even some Russians, notably a saturnine trio who kept much to themselves and played a great deal of chess, Lenin, Trotsky and Lunacharsky. Sooner or later most of the artists, writers and intelligentsia of Paris turned up at the little sidewalk tables, since those who stayed in Montmartre came to visit the expatriates, as the latter also, for some time to come, continued to return now and then for a party or a visit at their old habitat on the Butte.

Utrillo, with his addiction to Montmartre, came to Montparnasse infrequently; but when he did he usually managed to find his friend, and an escapade of some sort generally resulted. Fuss-Amore and des Ombiaux, in their book *Montparnasse*, tell of one night when Utrillo arrived at Rosalie's, a little restaurant whose proprietor, Rosalie Tobia, gave liberal credit to artists and thus built an admiring clientele, including Modigliani. Unaccountably, Utrillo had money, and he proceeded to order several drinks. The wine evidently made him nostalgic for Montmartre, for he sent Rosalie to buy some pastel sticks and, when she returned, he drew a scene from the Butte on one of the walls. He had barely finished when Modigliani came in. The two friends embraced and sat down to drink up the rest of Utrillo's funds. When they had done so they pressed Rosalie for credit, which she refused on the grounds that they were already drunk enough. A furious argument developed in Italian and French (Rosalie was from near Leghorn) and took an unexpected course when Modigliani wheeled on Utrillo to demand the return of a pair of trousers he had borrowed. Utrillo shouted that he would give them back only if Modigliani would return a coat that he had taken. They began to fight. The uproar attracted the police, who hauled them both off to jail. Sobered by this turn of affairs, they managed to talk their way to freedom and went off into the night, devotedly arm in arm, to look for something else to drink. Even such disgraceful episodes as this did not exhaust Rosalie's patience. She liked them both, and was exceptionally fond of Modigliani, who might well have gone hungry many nights except for her generosity. Over a period of years she acquired a large collection of his art, which she accepted in lieu of cash. It was an act of charity, and she put the paintings and drawings in the basement and forgot about them. The rats there ate paintings that today would have been worth many thousands of dollars.

Their last and climactic binge came in 1919 when Utrillo, having escaped from Picpus, and knowing that the authorities would be sure to look for him at Montmartre, headed instead for Montparnasse. It was early winter, but he had taken his chances regardless of the weather and had come away wearing only what he had on at the time, lightweight clothing and house slippers. He had no money. Luckily he managed to find Modigliani, who took him off at once to Rosalie's for a splendid meal, on credit, and then to the warm shelter of his little studio. Utrillo was in such good spirits that he painted two pictures, which Modigliani took off and sold for him. With the cash the friends set about celebrating their reunion, weaving noisily from bar to bar attended by a growing procession of curious and admiring youths of the district. At each stop Modigliani would introduce Maurice with a flourish as "the greatest painter in Paris. He can drink more than anybody." Maurice would answer modestly: "No, you are better. You can drink more." At last the money was gone, and the friends went to Modigliani's studio to sleep. When Modigliani awakened he found Utrillo gone—and also gone, he soon realized, was his coat, which Utrillo had taken off to a pawn shop so they could continue the party. Zborowski, Modigliani's patron and dealer, rescued the garment within a few hours, so the episode ended happily, with the friendship intact.

Such duties were minor and routine for Zborowski. This infinitely kind and patient man was as unique in his way as were any of the lurid characters he aided. A Polish poet who came to Paris in 1913 and settled in Montparnasse, he lived meagerly on his writings for several years and might have been remembered, if at all, as a minor figure of the era. One night, however, when he was at Foujita's flat with some friends, Modigliani's name came up. Fernande, a former streetwalker who had become Foujita's mistress and manager, turned to Zborowski with the sudden idea that he try to sell some of Modigliani's paintings for him. Zborowski admired Modigliani's work and thought it a pity that his dissipations and his studied tactlessness with dealers and customers kept him impoverished; and as he himself had time to spare, he took up the suggestion. It was impossible, of course, to control Modigliani; but Zborowski, with amazing devotion and self-sacrifice, thereafter protected him from the worst consequences of his faults, kept him supplied with materials and enough money for food and shelter, nursed him when he was ill, took him to the Riviera for nearly a year in 1918-19 for his health, and gradually established him in a minor way as an artist whose works had value. At times he even pawned his own clothes and personal effects to keep his difficult protégé in funds. And as if Modigliani were not a full-time problem, Zborowski, with inexhaustible good will, later began to act as good shepherd to several other disorderly artists, among them the fantastic Chaim Soutine, who for a time shared living quarters with Modigliani. It was thus in character for Zborowski to befriend Utrillo. Following the escapade of the pawned coat he took him to an obscure little hotel in Montparnasse, where he could remain hidden from the asylum authorities. There he supplied him with food and other necessities and with plenty of painting materials and kept him under his protection and care for several months. Utrillo behaved well and worked hard—until at last the familiar weaknesses reasserted themselves, with the usual consequences, and he was returned to Picpus.

Modigliani died in 1920. He had contracted tuberculosis at the age of seventeen, and, although the disease was arrested then and lay dormant for a number of years, his mode of life was bound to bring a recurrence. It took a slow course, and such was his vitality that he was able to work and to continue in a way of life that would have killed most healthy men. The disease was not, in the end, the direct cause of death, but a contributing factor through the generally lowered resistance it created. A particularly hallucinated night of drugging and drinking, ending with hours of exposure in the cold and rain, gave him pulmonary meningitis, and it was from this and alcoholic poisoning and possibly the complicating effect of drugs that he died. His last and true love, Jeanne Hébuterne, mother of a child by him and near confinement with a second, the next morning leaped from a window and killed herself.

A few of his friends formed a committee to raise funds

for the funeral. In death his perversities were forgiven: it seemed that everyone wanted to contribute. The funeral was a huge occasion, with carts of flowers and an outpouring of mourners—artists, models, frame-makers, dealers, supply merchants, café owners, waiters, prostitutes, singers, poets, and all the other mixed tribe of Bohemia—from both Montmartre and Montparnasse. Only his best friend, Utrillo, was missing.

CHAPTER EIGHT
SUCCESS AND DESPERATION

During all these twisted years—in and out of institutions, sometimes hiding from the police, his mother and Utter, or his own demons—Utrillo painted. Indeed, his output would have been extraordinary for anyone in the best health, and for one in his condition it was fantastic. In the war years he produced about a thousand paintings and drawings, an average of one every day and a half. He had an extraordinary visual memory, and he had besides a carefully collected file of postcards, snapshots, and newspaper pictures. They gave him the factual substance of his scenes, which he then molded and colored to suit himself. This is sometimes thought discreditable to him as an artist; but the fact is that Manet, Degas, and many others worked often from photographs, and for essentially the same reason—that it is not the substance of a painting, but the manipulation of elements by the individuality of the artist, that results in a work of art. In Utrillo's case particularly the subject matter was merely a means of personal expression. It should not be surprising that so many of his pictures "look alike," for in most of them he was saying, again and again, the same thing. He painted some wonderful pictures of churches, some of streets in Paris and nearby villages, but his favorite subject, the one he painted obsessively and insistently, remained Montmartre.

And at last real recognition began to come. In December of 1919, an exhibition at Lepoutre's gallery of his work from 1910 to 1915 achieved a good deal of success. Albert Flamant wrote the preface for the catalogue, and composed a sentence that was much quoted: "The Montmartre and the streets of Utrillo are but a dustcloth, but the embroidery that he puts on them for those who know how to look!" Adolphe Tabarant devoted an article to him in *Œuvre.* From this time on, perhaps reflecting the beginnings of success, his colors became brighter and more alive. In 1919, at a sale of Octave Mirbeau's collection, a Utrillo brought 1,000 francs. The next year at the liquidation of Louis Libaude's collection, Utrillo's "La rue du Mont Cenis" went for 2,700 francs. In 1921 there was an exhibition of his and Valadon's works at the well-known Weill gallery, and later that year Francis Carco published a little book about him in a series called "New French Painters." Soon all the dealers were after him, skillfully egged on by Utter, whose real forte was business. The money began to pour in. Utter, blandly telling of his own role later, referred to Utrillo as "the best commercial deal that had come up in half a century."

In 1922 there was another exhibition at Weill's, followed by one at Paul Guillaume's; in April of 1923, another at Weill's, and then, in May, a show organized by Paul Poiret, the couturier, who had become an admirer and who, because of his position as an arbiter of taste and fashion, thereby established Utrillo firmly as not merely a good painter but one whose works it was chic to own. The next month Bernheim-Jeune, then perhaps the leading gallery of Paris, mounted a Utrillo and Valadon exhibition and signed a contract with them for their future output, giving them a guaranteed joint income of 1,000,000 francs a year (then about $50,000). Most satisfying of all, the Druet gallery, where Maurice had been turned away in 1910 (and where Francis Jourdain had noticed him) now pleaded to be allowed to show his paintings.

By 1924, somewhat less than five years after the first solid recognition of his talent, there was no longer the slightest doubt of success. He was a celebrity whose name was known throughout Paris; dealers were searching the *bistros* and art supply shops, cafés and wine shops and all the other places in Montmartre where he might have traded paintings; the critics were arguing about which had been the first to realize his genius. Essentially he was untouched by it all. Money as such had no meaning for him, and fame, after all the previous neglect, merely reinforced a sense of irony that had grown within him. To be respected was a strange experience, and it took a long time for him to accept himself at the new value that others placed on him. He alternated between mockery and elation—and suspicion. "You see that pair over there?" he would confide, pointing to Suzanne and Utter. "I have to work all the time to support them." Walking down the street, he would pass to the other side when he came to a sidewalk café, and explain: "All those people stare at me. They think I'm crazy." And in fact, of course, he was only half sane. In 1921 he had had another internment at Saint Anne's. Early in 1924 he went again, this time voluntarily, to the private sanitarium of Ivry, where he stayed all spring. Meantime the biggest and most publicized exhibition of all opened at Bernheim-Jeune. He came back to the rue Cortot, to the old scenes and the old life with Suzanne and Utter; and one night soon afterward came the episode, already mentioned, when he was delivered home by the police after he had tried to dash his brains out against the walls of a jail cell.

He never had tried suicide before. Now, at this moment of triumph and deepest despair, Suzanne made a genuine effort for his salvation. For some years she had kept a certain number of his paintings from the market, so that they could be sold and money raised in a hurry if need be. With the great rise in value of his work this nest egg had grown to be worth a modest fortune. In

1923, she and Utter had traded some of the paintings for the Château de Saint-Bernard near Lyons, 350 miles southeast of Paris; and she decided to take him there and devote herself to nursing him back to health. That autumn she and Utter put him in a car, with his head still bandaged, and moved south. He was installed in a little room with a good view of the surrounding fields and woods. He had an iron bed, a straw chair, and an easel. For several months he lived in a semicoma, responding only to take food, to see after his own elementary needs, and to walk a bit in the château grounds and the nearby fields. It was the role of an ambulatory patient in a hospital. He was under constant watch by Suzanne or the servants, was kept from the household wine, given no money, and allowed at the nearby village only in the company of someone from the house.

Gradually he improved. He began to paint again—not country scenes, but the remembered scenes of Montmartre. At the end of the year he was allowed to go back again to Paris for a few days. The dealer Hodebert had arranged an exhibition of more than sixty of the white period (1908-1914) paintings. Utrillo walked about the rooms, looked at the pictures, rubbed his hands and left without saying a word.

It was during these and the many months that followed at the château that religion entered his life as a strong new element. He had had only the most cursory religious instruction as a child. Madeleine had had a peasant's faith, which was more superstition than religion; and Suzanne, growing up in the rebellious and free-thinking community of the Montmartre art world, found no attractions in the Church and had let him absorb only what might come his way. As a result he had acquired two preoccupations which were, however, less religious in meaning than they were symbolic of the needs of his peculiar personality. One of these was churches—never the interiors, never associated with services or processions or any other religious activities, but only the buildings themselves. He painted them often; and whether they were cathedrals or simple village chapels, under his brush they shared an extraordinary quality of serene dignity; they lived, just as the raggle-taggle buildings of Montmartre lived quite apart from the few sketchily indicated figures in the canvases. His other preoccupation was Saint Joan. In 1913 he had found and bought a little gilded statuette of her in the bazaar at Saint Sulpice, and thereafter carried it in his pocket everywhere with him. He would take it out and talk to it, telling it his troubles, and at night he would put it beside his bed. He brought it with him to the château, and in those early months of convalescence it was his only confidante. He would contemplate it for long hours at a time, and sometimes would write poems to the saintly memory of the miraculous girl who had led France through so many tribulations.

One day at the château he found and began to read a

Catechism that belonged to his nurse's child. The sound of the words and the beauty of the simple religious teachings had a profound effect. He demanded a Bible, and for the next weeks immersed himself in the Psalms and parables. He became addicted to these new discoveries in almost the sense that he had been addicted to alcohol. It was not an evangelical faith—he pressed it on no one else—but a matter of deep personal hunger which demanded satisfaction in endless reading of the Bible, the Catechism and the Prayer Book and in solitary prayer. It was with the two obsessions, the old one of Montmartre and the new one of religion, that he lived out the time that lay before him at Saint-Bernard.

Suzanne did her best to take proper care of him, and for a matter of months her devotion was steady and selfless. But she was incapable of consistency; and as he improved, she allowed herself the familiar delusion that he was on the road to real recovery, and with mounting optimism she set about attending to the many and always fascinating details of her independent career. She had not attained (nor would she ever) the public and commercial success of her son, but on her own merits, as well as through association with him in a number of exhibitions, she had made a distinguished name. In 1921, when she showed at the Galerie Levy and the Galerie Weill, the critics had been more than generous. Tabarant had written: "... under her brush, everything becomes animated and alive; this extraordinary woman is passion itself, and one seeks in vain to find someone to whom she can be compared." Warnod had said: ". . . Suzanne Valadon's nudes are painted on a scale that is so clear, so radiant that they enchant by the truth that emanates from them." Robert Rey wrote: "I wish to say and to say again that we have, in Suzanne Valadon, a very great artist. . . ." That year also she exhibited at the International Exposition at Geneva. New triumphs followed in the next years, until by 1924-25 she was securely established as one of the leading artists of her day.

Her joint success with Utrillo brought not merely prosperity, but a double portion of it, and in a dizzyingly short period of time. As unused to money as to fame, she found herself irresistibly impelled toward Paris, where she could enjoy the combination. She had kept the studio at the rue Cortot. At first she only visited there; finally, however, she only visited at Saint-Bernard, leaving Utrillo for long periods in the charge of the servants. She began to indulge old ambitions and new whims. She bought an expensive car and hired a chauffeur, whom she dressed in a livery of white flannel. If the car was busy or in repair when she had a sudden desire to go to the château, she took a taxi. Several such times she was so overcome with delight on arriving that she told the taxi driver to wait at the inn nearby, and then quite forgot about him while his charges rolled up for a day or two. She had always wanted an astrakhan coat. Now she bought one, and was so charmed when her two big dogs one day found it on the floor and went to sleep on it that afterward she shared it with them—it became their bed when she was not wearing it. The dogs ate *filet mignon,* which she had especially cooked for them at her favorite restaurants. She had always loved to entertain. Now she became a hostess on a grand scale, serving crowds of her friends with extravagant buffets at the studio and with choice meals and wines at the gayest restaurants. She loved flowers (some of her best pictures are flower studies) and with the new wealth she could afford as many as she wanted. Often she wanted all of them: she would enter a florist shop and in breathless pleasure order this . . . and that . . . and those *beautiful* ones, until she had bought the whole stock to be delivered to the studio. She spent money wildly, lent it without question, and gave it away in fantastic amounts to beggars, waiters, taxi drivers, or anyone else who struck her sympathy or who had done her a service. Somehow, even so, there was enough left so that in 1926 she could buy a house on the rue Junot in a rather bourgeois neighborhood of Montmartre.

Her anxiety for Maurice continued. But, like everything else in her quixotic temperament, it was recorded either in huge bursts or not at all. One day it would consume her and she would hurry to Saint-Bernard to encourage and console him, or, as he regained his health, perhaps to bring him back to Montmartre for a visit.

The next day or next week she might be so immersed in a new painting, a future exhibition, a party to give or attend that she would seem to have forgotten everything but the project of the moment.

Aside from her concern for Maurice there was another blemish in a life that otherwise was filled with satisfactions. Utter was misbehaving on a grand scale. His actions in the earlier years of their arrangement had been perhaps no more than Suzanne took for granted: his drinking, his narcotics, his infidelities, his occasional rages against her were manifestations of the same temperament to which she had been attracted. The change came at about the time she and Utrillo achieved their first real successes—successes for which Utter was to a considerable extent responsible. Temperamentally an artist, he was endowed by nature to be a businessman. Not that he was a bad artist; but with his ruddy cheeks and merry eyes and little blond beard, his easy conversation and reassuring manner, and above all his sharp ability to negotiate, he was much better as an artists' agent; and this, in effect, was what he became. He continued to paint large numbers of pictures that nobody wanted, living meanwhile mostly at the rue Cortot studio, but much of his time was given to making profitable arrangements with dealers on behalf of Suzanne and Utrillo. But for one who had instructed and then married the first, and protected and pitied the other, it was a situation bound to carry the seeds of discontent. As his commercial creations grew, so did his reactions against them. He drank more; he philandered constantly; he beat Suzanne and mocked Utrillo; he spent money extravagantly and ran up bills. One day, when Suzanne called for the car, he announced that he had sold it because he needed the cash. All of this had a morbid effect on Utrillo, and perhaps contributed to the attempted suicide and extraordinary breakdown that occurred in 1924. As for Suzanne, who had begun to drink very heavily also, she could forgive Utter's alcoholic excesses as she could forgive his spendthrift ways. But she did not enjoy the beatings that he increasingly gave her in their drunken arguments, and above all she could not forgive his flagrant sexual adventures. She was old now, sixty-one years old, twenty-one years older than he. Only traces of her beauty remained. She could not bear the thought that the money she earned by her painting should go to finance his attentions to younger women. In 1926 she left him at the rue Cortot studio and moved to the newly acquired house on the rue Junot.

Even so, she kept him on an allowance and saw him often both at the house and the studio. Now and again, when she brought Utrillo back from the château, they would all join in a family reunion. Gradually Utrillo was allowed to spend the winter months in Paris. But as her own alcoholism increased Suzanne became a less reliable guardian for him, until at last something resembling the previous state of affairs developed. Utrillo did not drink as much, but Suzanne and Utter drank more. A visitor remembers one typical night scene at the rue Cortot. The place was littered with bottles, old paint tubes, discarded canvases, cigarette butts, and remnants of food. A great deal of wine and liquor had been drunk. An argument began among the three of them—about what, or who against whom, was not clear. Their voices rose, a bottle hurtled across the room and shattered against the wall with a crash that brought a moment of silence. Utrillo began to scream. . . .

They were all too old to change. The years passed, illumined by such scenes: the same eccentricities, jealousies, extravagances and remorse. There were times of peace, and on the whole Utrillo's mental condition improved, beginning noticeably after Suzanne moved to the rue Junot. The tragic element left his pictures, and the colors became increasingly sharp and gay. He lived with her during the winter. In the good weather they went to the château. And there in the autumn of 1929 came an extraordinary testimonial to "le peintre" who now, twenty years after that derisive compliment, had become "le peintre" in all seriousness. The French government awarded him the Cross of the Legion of Honor. A delegation of artists and writers came to present it. One of them has remembered: "The painter sat on a low wall during the simple ceremony, playing with the yellow leaves that drifted down, twirling his hat. When it was over, Utrillo murmured a few words. His mother, Suzanne Valadon, cried and expressed her gratitude. That was all."

This family portrait, typical of Valadon's work in its bold execution and heavy outlining of the figures, was painted in 1912 and shows (left to right) Utter, Valadon, Utrillo, and Madeleine. Maurice, in a familiar pose, was then in his great "white period."

This was Maurice's costume as an eleven-year-old schoolboy.

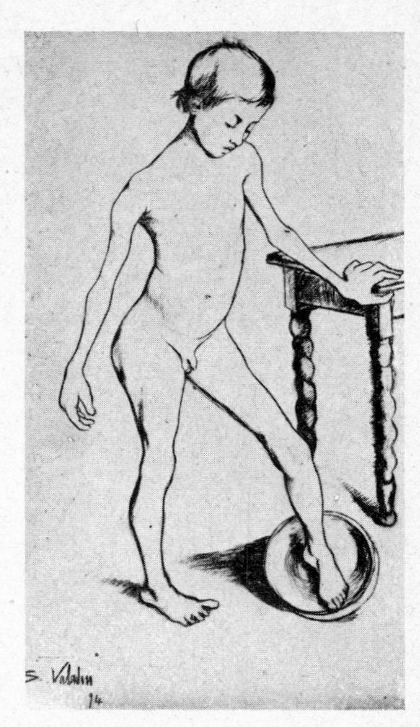

Suzanne's drawing of Maurice at the same age.

The atelier at 12 rue Cortot was shared by Suzanne, Maurice, and André Utter for many years. The portrait of Maurice at left was done by Utter. It is now in the Utrillo-Valadon room of the Museum of Modern Art in Paris.

Valadon a few years before her death still had traces of her former beauty. Her health was impaired, never her spirit.

Valadon drew this sketch of Utter when he was twenty-three and they were at the beginning of their relationship.

Valadon's facility with line and her power of characterization are evident in this head of Maurice, done in 1910. He was then at liberty between two of his many "cures."

"Gaby-the-Brunette" worked for Valadon as model and housemaid, and nearly became Maurice's bride. But she fled when the time drew near and was not seen again.

he House of Mimi Pinson," a good white-period picture done in 1914, shows Utrillo's eoccupation with the qualities of texture and design afforded by the old walls and jumbled buildings and three-dimensional streets of Montmartre.

Le Lapin Agile, fronting the cemetery of St. Vincent and flanked by a vineyard, a favorite subject and a favorite resort in Utrillo's youth.

Arrests were so common in Utrillo's life that, lapsing momentarily into the role of genre painter, he did this scene of himself being led away.

Mme. Utrillo retains a sense of theater acquired during her days as an ingénue. This picture was taken during one of the rare trips to Montmartre she allows Maurice.

Utrillo, during this same outing, visited Le Lapin Agile, where he stared about in excitement, then drew in the guest book and was given wine by the grateful proprietor.

Utrillo goes several times a day to pray in his private chapel, which stands close behin his house at Le Vesinet. Along with other religious figures it contains several statuettes St. Joan. One can be seen on the altar at left.

CHAPTER NINE

LUCIE PAUWELS' GREAT AWAKENING

In the early 1930's Suzanne's health began to fail. She was in her mid-sixties, and had lived robustly for fifty years. Now, with age and sustained abuse, her body began to lose its recuperative powers. In 1935 uremic poisoning set in and she was taken to the American Hospital in Neuilly. She was a bad patient. She was terrified of the prospect of death, and equally terrified of the treatments which might prevent it. The doctors and nurses made her uneasy; she screamed when they approached her with a medical instrument and fought them off. She was extravagantly gay on good days; she solicited pity and love, engaged visitors in probing conversations as to whether they thought she had a chance to recover; she was herself. When she was not wholly preoccupied with her illness her thoughts turned to what was to become of Maurice.

There was no doubt in her mind that she had been a

good mother. She could look back over the years and tell herself, or any listener, how often she had rescued him from his weakness, how many times she had sent him to the best doctors, how she had sacrificed her own work to care for him. There was truth in everything she said—enough, at least, to furnish the material for a legend that began to grow soon after Utrillo's first great successes and still survives, the legend of a devoted mother who through love and attention preserved the genius of an afflicted son. Having created the legend, she believed in it so sincerely that during these final years she made it come true. It would be too much to say that she changed her way of life. She never lost her quixotic ways or her joy in pure experience or her capacity for excitement; but there was pride and a measure of real devotion in her attitude toward Maurice. And the fact was quite apparent that he needed someone to look after him. She regretted now more than ever that he had never found a wife.

She could tell herself that in this, too, she had done her best for him. Having, as she did, a wholehearted acceptance of sex as an elemental necessity of life, she had been puzzled by the minor interest it evidently had for him. Within the milieu of Montmartre it was inevitable that he would make experiments; but according to the "autobiography" he composed at M. Gay's, his first experience with a woman did not come until 1911, when he was twenty-eight, and he records that his reaction was one of shame. Afterward he had casual liaisons, mostly with prostitutes, but sometimes with girls procured by Suzanne, who brought them to the studio in hopes that a mutual attraction would lead to a natural result. Most of these efforts failed, for either he paid the girls no attention or made such a scene that they left immediately. In 1915 there was a close brush with matrimony with a girl remembered only as "Gaby-the-Brunette," who worked for Suzanne as a model and part-time maid. She was a big, fleshy woman, as one can see from the nudes Suzanne painted of her, and she appealed to Maurice, whose taste ran to her type. Evidently she was fond of him, or at least treated him kindly, and she was so good-natured that it was hard for her to refuse any suggestion. When, through Suzanne's manipulations, she found herself engaged to Maurice, she passively accepted the situation until shortly before the wedding, when she disappeared. Maurice was sorry to find her no longer in the studio, but not disappointed at remaining a bachelor. Thereafter he never was close to marriage, although it remained a possibility that theoretically he desired and sometimes talked about with an appearance of real yearning.

He was married in 1936. Mme. Utrillo, the former Lucie Pauwels, a short, stout woman of exceptional vigor and personality, told this part of the story to me during several interviews in the summer of 1949. She told it very well, and I can do no better than to quote her:

"I have always been extremely gifted. I came from a wonderful family, the de Veaus of Angoulême, and as a child I recited poetry so beautifully that it was decided I should be an actress. I was always called in when great artists came to play in the city. The great Coquelin heard me one day and said immediately, 'There is a girl who should be on the stage.' Of course he was very, very old then and I was very young. If I had stayed on the stage there is absolutely no question that I would have been the greatest actress in France. A palmist saw my hand one day and said that there were only two others like it that had ever existed. One was the hand of Sarah Bernhardt and the other George Sand.

"I came to Paris for study in the theater and soon played the lead in *Tartuffe* in a company that gave over three hundred performances in Switzerland, Paris and Belgium. It was at the Théâtre de la Parque in Brussels that M. Pauwels was in the audience and admired me from afar. That very night I met him at a splendid reception given for us in Brussels. And then I didn't see him again. But *six months* later I was again in Paris and dining in the Bois when, suddenly, amidst ohing and ahing of admiration, there drove up the most wonderful-looking man in a beautiful carriage. It was M. Pauwels! He remembered me at once and told me again how beautiful I was. From that time on we saw a great deal of each other. He was from a Belgian banking family, but was born in Paris. He spoke many languages without accent. He was distinguished, aristocratic, interested in everything: fine horses, flowers, birds, also stuffed birds. Did you see the stuffed white parakeet on the piano? M. Pauwels! He collected paintings including Utrillos and his name was well known in all the artistic circles. So when he asked me to marry him, but under one condition, that I give up the theater, I agreed willingly because I knew that this marriage was one of real distinction.

"In the winter of 1919 M. Pauwels and I went up to Montmartre to look for Suzanne Valadon and Utrillo. We didn't know where they lived. I told M. Pauwels to go one way and I would go the other and we would see what success we had. I had taken only a few steps down a little street when suddenly I saw approaching me a tiny little woman, looking a little like a jockey, with a portfolio of drawings under her arm. I approached her and said, 'Excuse me, Madame, but are you not the painter, Suzanne Valadon?' Mme. Valadon smiled very warmly and replied, 'I am, but I don't think I know you.' I smiled and answered, 'No, you wouldn't know me, my name is Mme. Pauwels, and . . .' Suzanne Valadon's eyes opened wide and she exclaimed, 'Not the wife of *the* M. Pauwels, whose name is on the lips of all the artists in Montmartre!'

"I quickly called my husband and we all went together, that very night, to the studio on the rue Cortot of Suzanne Valadon, André Utter, and Maurice Utrillo. When we entered, Maurice was in the traditional pose for which he is so famous, elbow on the knee, face in palm of hand, eyes gazing at the floor. When he looked up I could see a flash of admiration go over his face. But he was too well-bred to do anything about it. After we left that night Maurice said to his mother, his eyes filled with longing, 'Send me, send me a wife like Mme. Pauwels!'

"From that day on I used to go very often to Suzanne Valadon's house and she and I became very close friends. I used to see them all, Utter, Utrillo and Valadon. I can tell you that Utter was a very attractive man, full of health, but despicable; he used to go on sprees with his friends and they would get drunk and pick up one girl after another. And Suzanne was a wonderful painter but she didn't know how to bring up children.

"Well, in 1933 M. Pauwels died. I didn't know what to do. You have no idea what it is like to have been held up and supported by such a wonderful man and then, suddenly, to have him no more. He was only fifty-two when he died. I didn't know what to do with myself. I was not old, but I wasn't young, and although I wasn't thinking about another husband I wondered what the future would bring. M. Pauwels left me quite well off, even though he had suffered reverses a few years before, but I certainly didn't have enough to live in great comfort for the rest of my life. I went to Angoulême and stayed there for a while with two of my oldest friends—two widows, you can imagine what the atmosphere was like. I used to come to Paris once in a while, but I didn't enjoy it much. I was too anxious to know what the future would bring me.

"You know, when I first met Utrillo he was so enamored of me, by my grace and beauty, but being a gentleman he couldn't say anything because I was still married to M. Pauwels. But, two years after my first husband died, I received so many beautiful love letters from Maurice. The first one said, 'Are you still your *suave*'—that is what he called me—'*suave* and beautiful self and can you come to see us?' He was living at the château then and it was a terrible life for him, because Valadon and Utter were never there and he was shut up pretty much by himself under the care of a nurse.

"Across the street from my apartment in Paris I had often noticed a sign hanging from a window—it was a carved wooden hand. I had no idea what it meant; I even thought it could possibly be for a manicurist. But one day a friend of mine told me that the woman who lived there was one of the greatest clairvoyants in Paris. I didn't believe in such things, but I was so anxious to know, in any way, what was going to become of me that I asked her to come to my house. She read both my hand and the cards. The minute she cut the cards she said, 'You are a widow, but in two years you will be married again. Your first marriage was one of the most brilliant in all Paris and he was a wonderful man, but your next marriage will be with one of the greatest men in all of France.' I didn't know anyone at that time, I had been so shut up from the world, and even when she said, 'He usually dresses in gray-blue and you'll be surrounded by paintings,' Utrillo didn't enter my mind. Then she took hold of my wrist and said, 'His first name is Maurice.' I ran through all the Maurices I knew, but none was great and the only one I didn't think of was Maurice Utrillo.

"I went to see another clairvoyant, an old woman in Angoulême. She told me the same thing, and also said that she saw me in a hospital with a lot of angels around. When I returned to Paris, I had been there only a few days when Suzanne Valadon's chauffeur came to get me, saying that Mme. Valadon was ill and in the American Hospital at Neuilly. Of course I went to her. She was in a very bad condition. Her recovery took a long time, and I went to see her almost every day. While she was still in danger of death she said to me, 'What will happen to my poor Maurice? Who will take care of him?'

"Then it came to me, like a great awakening, and I saw that *he* was the greatest man living in France and that *he* was the man I was going to marry!"

CHAPTER TEN
SUZANNE'S LAST DAYS

Following this revelation, Lucie took things into her capable hands. Soon afterward she went with Utrillo to dinner, and before the evening was over he had proposed. He had to produce his military card in order to get a license, and it developed that Suzanne had thrown it out long ago. Luckily he remembered the date and serial number, and Lucie soon got a duplicate. She wanted a church wedding as well as a civil one, but Utrillo had never been baptized. In short order he was baptized, confirmed, and had made his first communion. Because of Suzanne's wild way with finances he had no money for an engagement present or wedding ring, but Lucie found a metalsmith who traded the rings as well as a silver cigarette case for a small painting. Utrillo's clothes were a disgrace, for although he had plenty of them everything was soiled and in disrepair. Lucie cleaned and mended the pants of the suit he was to be married in.

Meantime Suzanne had been released from the hospital and was back at the rue Junot. The coming marriage affected her oddly. "You know," Lucie recalls, "Suzanne Valadon, all the time I knew her, right up until a few days before my marriage with Maurice, was one of my best friends. But then she became very jealous of me. When she saw we really were going to get married, she wanted no more of us and kept saying, 'Well, if you're going to get married, go on and get out of here.' I said that we had waited up to this point and that we might as well wait a few more days, and have the ceremony and then leave, but I can tell you it wasn't a very comfortable feeling."

The civil wedding took place on April 18, 1935 at the *mairie* of the 16th *arrondissement*, and was performed by a former classmate of Maurice's from the College Rollin. The church ceremony followed soon afterward at Angoulême; "almost in secret," Lucie remembers, "because I knew that if it were made too well known at least thirty thousand people would have wanted to come." For the next year they stayed in Angoulême, where Lucie devoted herself to the functions of wife and police matron. She let Utrillo paint only a little, and meantime allowed none of his paintings to be sold. Word spread that he was finished as a painter, that he was too ill to work and that, in any case, the normalcy of the life Lucie imposed on him could only ruin his inspiration. As a result, the value of his existing paintings quadrupled, and when finally she began to release new ones she got such good prices that she was able to buy a substantial villa at Le Vésinet, a rich suburb of Paris. Here they moved in 1937.

Suzanne lived on at the rue Junot house, and Utter stayed at the rue Cortot. They maintained their same half-married, half-separated, affectionate and quarrelsome relationship. Utter, no longer needed as an agent, gave himself entirely to painting, but was no more successful than before. He was embittered and cynical. Suzanne kept him on an allowance, but as Lucie now had full control over Utrillo's income Suzanne's scale of living declined and with it, necessarily, Utter's. Suzanne stayed mostly at home, for she never regained her full strength after the illness. She painted mostly flower studies now, and spent many hours at this work during the months when her garden was in bloom. She came to Le Vésinet occasionally, and Lucie and Maurice visited her. She taught painting, and among her pupils were a few, such as Odette Dumoret and Pierre Noyelle, who went on to make modest reputations for themselves. She entertained now and then, but lived a great deal among her memories.

On April 7, 1938, she felt ill and called Mme. Kvpil and Mme. Poulbot, wives of the painters, for help. But it was too late: she had had a severe stroke. She died that same day. Two days later she was buried from the little Church of Saint Peter that sits at the top of the Butte Montmartre.

Maurice at first was numb and almost insane with grief. He made a surprisingly quick recovery, however, and after a time began to paint again. He consecrated a room at Le Vésinet to her memory, and hung it with as many of her drawings and paintings as he could find. Every day he went there to contemplate her remembered presence, and to pray.

He had written a number of poems to her during her lifetime. This one is typical:

To My Mother

Suzanne Valadon, my mother is thus named.
She is a noble woman, as beautiful as she is good
In virtue, in beauty. In a word, a goddess of genius
In addition, endowed with His divine breath.

Then, He did not share the place among the false ones
In order that she could attain
Summits defying humans
Where enthroned are the masters, alone the pure, a very few.

With a firm and sure brush, defying matter,
She enchants, she animates the sky, flowers, stones.
Houses have a soul, their profound secrets
She embellishes in spite of what the Beaux-Arts decree.

The personality is so great, so pure
Of this superwoman in human form
That the most troubled face, the most enigmatic laugh
Is understood and transmitted to her canvas.

In magic colors, in natural integrated tones,
Heavy colors, pinks, painting the whites, sepia for Negroes

(Negresses to be more exact) O how many paintings!
How many famous subjects, titanic works!

To say all in a word, she to my modesty
From her breast gives me life and exquisiteness
From her noble art ahead of its time, she fulfills my wishes,
She whom I love, adore, O with a pious love.

Maurice, Utrillo, V.

CHAPTER ELEVEN
A NEW LIFE

The two events, the marriage and his mother's death so soon afterward, revolutionized Utrillo's manner of life. Left in full authority, Lucie established him in an ironclad and antiseptic regimen that has rarely varied in the years since.

The house at Le Vésinet is called "La Bonne Lucie." To anyone familiar with Utrillo's former existence it is an astonishing place. Of confectioner's pink stucco with a dove-gray trim, it sits at the foot of a garden of neat rectangular lawns, potted plants, small trees and crushed stone walks, decorated with lifelike ceramics of frogs and turtles and two large marble statues of classic figures. On one side of the garden is a dog run for the prize Pekinese which Lucie raises and on which she lavishes loud affection. On the other is a large aviary containing fifty parakeets of a variety developed by M. Pauwels in his days as a bird fancier. The house furnishings are ornate and varied, with a sumptuous use of gilding, carving, and tapestry. The main sitting room is dominated by two large murals of Montmartre by Utrillo and a three-foot statue of Joan of Arc. Here and there on the walls, printed in gold leaf, is a series of mottoes and sentiments such as:

> One must do as well as he can without going beyond the esteemed powers.

and

> Everything that you give, flowers, everything that you keep, rots.

and

> Everything here reflects a priceless presence.
> Here, calm happiness marries silence.
> All here is ordained, alive, harmonious.
> Dreams capture you in the image of God.
> It is here that they have linked in love their two lives
> In the shadow of genius.

The house contains several dozen paintings by Utrillo and an almost equal number by Lucie, who began to paint a few years ago. She signs her canvases "Lucie Valore," her stage name, and customarily refers to herself in that way. "Lucie Valore, Maurice Utrillo, Suzanne Valadon—none of them had any training in painting," she says. "It is truly incredible!" She paints in a primitive style, with crudely drawn figures and bright, flat colors, and her work is widely unappreciated. She knows how often great talent goes unnoticed, however, and is not discouraged. "As a painter I kneel before Suzanne Valadon," she has said. "She is much greater than I am. But of course the future will tell how great I am going to be, and the future will choose, that is the way I feel." A few years ago she added a square tower on an upper corner of the house, and there, with a view commanding the garden, directly in line with the heavy doors that are the sole entry to the walled domain, she spends several hours a day at her easel. This connects with her bedroom below, a large room decorated with three of Utrillo's paintings and six of hers, along with various *objets d'art*, including a statuette of Napoleon and two painted urns showing Napoleon in battle scenes. Beneath her window, in a little squared-off and neatly planted garden plot, is a statue of the Muse of Painting, palette in hand. She found it at a second-hand dealer's, and for having salvaged it from this fate felt entitled to dedicate it to herself. The history of the rescue is inscribed around the base, and since the sentence ends with her name, and turns a corner at that point, "Lucie Valore" in huge letters is all that can be seen when one looks at the statue from the front.

Across the street from La Bonne Lucie, bought with money realized from the sale of the house on rue Junot after Suzanne's death, is a large enclosed garden which furnishes the household with flowers, berries and vegetables. Lucie has a small summerhouse there decorated with mementos of her past life: a large oil of herself when she was Mme. Pauwels and relics of M. Pauwels himself—pictures of him driving a coach and four, driving a smart rig, a scale model of one of his carriages. Amid these evocative surroundings she often has tea, receives dealers and visitors, and works over her correspondence and accounts. She supervises every detail of Utrillo's business affairs, and scrutinizes every expenditure with the eye of a cashier. In contrast to the days when any unscrupulous dealer could trade a bottle of wine for a picture, or any friend could rely on half of whatever was in Utrillo's pocket, a matter involving the possibility of money is now subjected to long diplomatic negotiation. One of the first victims of the change was André Utter who, after Suzanne's death, expected that the allowance he had received from her would be continued by Maurice. When, after a short tapering-off period, Lucie stopped it entirely, he was furious. He lived by his wits for the next few years and then, during the war, went to stay at the château, where the garden helped with food and the lands gave him some income. After the war he sold the place, and was able to live well again on the proceeds until his death in 1947.

As a result of such sensible management by Lucie, Utrillo is wealthy now. He has been able to buy her a double rope of pearls and several extraordinarily large diamond-crusted rings. Her clothes come from the leading couturiers of Paris; not, she has explained, because of any vanity on her part but because "I must dress in keeping with my name as the wife of the greatest painter in France."

The whole scene pleases her almost beyond her powers to describe. "How wonderful it is for him here," she has said. "What a change for the master, my little Maurice, my genius! And it is I, Lucie Valore, who has done it all. I am the Joan of Arc!"

At first Utrillo sometimes seemed rebellious under her care. He would slip away to the village to look for wine, but scouting parties always found him before much damage was done. Once, in 1941, he escaped entirely. Lucie has recalled: "I was sitting at the window of my studio in the tower one evening, an August night at the beginning of the war, when all of a sudden I noticed that the front gate was open. A terrible thought went through my head—I *knew* that Maurice had gone off. I looked all over the house and began to call, 'Maurice! Maurice! Maurice!' But there was no answer. The servants and I ran up and down the street in front of the house. I went across to the two English ladies who used to live nearby and asked them if they had seen him. They hadn't, but they joined us in the search. We called all the bars and all the police stations in all the surrounding towns. To no avail! We telephoned steadily until three in the morning but no one had seen him. Finally I went to bed in such a terrible state. I felt that I would never see my Maurice again, my wonderful genius, never again. Of course I didn't sleep at all.

"Toward the end of the next morning I saw the gate open and in walked one of those watchmen from the service that patrols this neighborhood. Cowering behind him was Maurice. He didn't dare come in. He was afraid of what I would do—that I would never let him come back. Poor little thing! Never let him come back! I have never been so happy to see anyone in my life. He had gone to a bar in the village and stayed there until ten o'clock, which was closing time, and then he paid for his drinks and started home. But he went in the wrong direction. He walks very fast, and the less familiar the road the more confused he became. After he had walked through the forest for a long time he came to a little cabin, and went in. There was a tramp sleeping there, and Utrillo went to sleep beside him. 'You know,' he told me, 'I had spent only a hundred francs on wine, so I made sure to sleep on the side where I carried the rest of my money so I wouldn't be robbed while I was asleep. But the next morning, when I awakened, I took it all out of my pocket and put it beside the sleeping tramp, saying, 'You will never know who left you this money.'

"On the way home he stopped to pray at the Eglise de Croissy, and that same day, later, he painted the church from memory, because of his gratitude to be back here again safely with me.

"Since that time we don't give him any money at all. I handle everything for him. Where could he have found a better manager? An artist who understands him and a clever manager besides. He never goes out alone any more, not even with me. When we go for a walk I take the manservant along. Maurice is apt to get very nervous sometimes, and I just turn him over to the servant. Also it makes a much better impression. After all, he's the great master, and it wouldn't do for him to go places by himself, or just with me. A while ago we went to the Hotel de Ville in Paris for a ceremony, and he walked with me, and then the secretary in back and then the chauffeur and manservant. It made a very good impression."

Life at La Bonne Lucie nowadays is broken only by such rare visits to Paris, an occasional drive in the countryside and two annual trips to the South during the months of harsh weather. One of these is to Dax, a spa northeast of Biarritz, where Lucie takes the waters; the other, in late winter and early spring, is to the Riviera. While at the latter, in 1949, they became acquainted with Prince Ali Khan and Rita Hayworth and were invited to the wedding of the glamorous figures. This thrilling relationship is memorialized in a large, heavily framed photograph on the piano, showing the two couples standing abreast in an attitude of gay camaraderie. "How exquisite and charming she is! And how handsome he is!" Lucie points out to visitors. "See how the Prince has his arm through mine. Did you notice?" To be present at the wedding, Lucie even delayed returning to La Bonne Lucie at the expense of personally supervising the spring care of the garden, a concession of some moment; for she loves flowers, and the garden is her chief avocation. With the dogs and birds, her painting and the supervision of Utrillo's affairs, her shopping trips and occasional dinners in Paris with old friends, it makes up her life.

One day in the garden, while picking roses, she was chatting with my wife and me about her marriage with Utrillo: "Everyone said it wouldn't last, but here we are now, married nearly fifteen years. When we had been married ten years I gave a big party and all the important people came out here and saw how wonderfully we were living. From now on we're going to give a party every five years—the time is growing too short now to do it every ten years. The last time we had at least 125 people, from the Comédie-Française and everywhere, and it will be a big affair next time, too. I know how surprised so many of them are that our marriage is still working so well. But you can put it down that anyone born in March, as I was, is a fighter."

Thereupon she cut a huge yellow rose and handed it to my wife, and, in a defenseless manner I could not have imagined, said quietly, "Of course, it has been a lonely life. He is not a husband for a woman."

Today, at sixty-eight, Maurice Utrillo is a small husk of a man with the tottering walk, the rheumy eyes, the skin folds, nervous tics and emaciated look of a Bowery character. He seems to live part of the time in a semi-coma; again, the mists partly clear, and he becomes almost animated, perhaps to the extent of making an ironic little joke, perhaps to raise his voice in a weak, hoarse shout and stamp his foot against some action or suggestion from those around him. His real feelings about his new milieu are difficult to know: they seem contradictory and are as formless and changeable as those of the very young or very old. Lucie is to him, one senses, a custodian rather than a person, and his attitude seems mainly one of weary resignation, with flashes of mockery, anger, defiance, and amused contempt—replaced in a moment, in any time of uncertainty or other strain, with panicky dependence. It is as if he believes that his whole existence, physical and mental, the whole pattern of his minutely organized life, might fly apart in irreparable and terrifying and fatal confusion except for the key element of her strong will. He has become even more obsessively religious, and every morning and evening spends an hour in the little chapel that has been built for him in back of the house. He has memorized the names of all the saints' days, and pays his respects to each in series around the calendar. Saint Joan still is his favorite. He has made pilgrimages both to Domremy, her birthplace, and Orléans, where she lived as a young girl. He still has the little gilded statuette of her, and has added other statues and medals. "Every day, many times, I kiss all my

Jeanne d'Arcs," he told a visitor. "It's hard work, but it's a saintly work." On Sundays, after the regular services are over and the people have left, he is driven to the nearby church of Saint Pauline, where a large statue of Saint Joan stands on a side altar. He sits in a chair directly in front of it, and spends an hour in solitary devotion. Almost all of his old friends are dead now, and on the anniversary of their deaths he prays for them: for M. Gay, and the amiable Marie Vizier, and Modigliani, Zborowski, and all the others. The anniversary of his grandmother's death is sacred. The day of Suzanne Valadon's death he spends in the chapel, praying until he passes into a state of exhaustion.

He still drinks—but it is heavily watered wine, and in quantities carefully supervised by Lucie and the three servants. "I couldn't take it away from him entirely," she says. "It's like a drug with him, and if he had none at all it would kill him." Like many old alcoholics, he has reached the state where even a small amount makes him mildly intoxicated.

And he still paints. He has a little back room that faces the chapel, and there, surrounded by his Jeanne d'Arcs and other religious objects, he works for about two hours each afternoon and for several hours each night. When he sits at the easel a transformation takes place, and the decrepit old man gives way to the confident artist. His hands are steady, and the long, thin fingers, as clean and scrubbed as a surgeon's, apply the strokes without hesitation. He finishes about a dozen pictures a year. Some of them are poor imitations of himself, but others are as deft and lovely as anything he has done since the white period. They are almost always scenes of Montmartre.

Not long ago he was asked whether he would like to live in Montmartre again. "The people there are all idiots—idiots!" he said. "I have consecrated myself to my painting and to my wife." Then, later, when Lucie had left the room, "There's not an hour that I don't think of it." And a little later: "I'm shut in out here and they won't let me go. I would rather be there than anywhere."

CHAPTER TWELVE
EPILOGUE

If the legend of Montmartre can be said to have begun in 1865 with Manet and his group of the Café Guerbois, its end can also be dated at 1935 when Utrillo was taken away. Artists still live on the Holy Hill, and perhaps among them is someone who will rise to overturn the canons of contemporary painting as Picasso, Cézanne, and Manet did in their times. But, if so, the genius has preferred to remain invisible; there is nothing in the air or in the places where pictures are displayed to suggest revolution. On a sunny Sunday, every other corner seems to sprout an artist—nearly all of them week-end amateurs hopeful, perhaps, that propinquity to the scene of past greatness will have an effect on their brushwork. Here and there, at almost any time of any day, one can also see a ragamuffin who might be Utrillo himself. But one has the feeling somehow that such people are hired by the day, like tea-room gypsies. The center of artistic creation—such as it is—in Paris these days is Montparnasse; and Montmartre in a literal sense has been abandoned to live off its past. Business is good. Nearly every door on the Place du Tertre leads to a restaurant or café. In the tourist season, the waiters cannot work fast enough to bring the coffees and *apéritifs* to the customers seated at the tables under the colored umbrellas that have replaced most of the trees. And in the evening, in every quarter of the Butte, Bohemians-for-a-night can frolic and drink and buy souvenirs to take home. To visit Montmartre now is a little like attending a carnival in a graveyard.

Progress, too, has come to Montmartre. The shack where Modigliani lived is now the site of a comfortable apartment house, and other modern structures, many of them in the peculiarly hideous "style moderne" of the 1920's, have replaced the quarters where Steinlen, Poulbot, Hector Berlioz, and many other remembered talents once unfolded. The rue Cortot has kept its cobblestones, along with the studios of No. 12 and a few others; but apartments and multifamily houses now line most of the street.

Yet, in spite of it all, Montmartre retains its distinctive character and a special charm. A great many of the old buildings and the old vistas remain. One can still trace Marie-Clémentine's path up the Butte from the rue du Poteau, and find the cafés where Renoir bought her a drink after a hard day's work at the studio. The little Moulin Joyeux near the Church of Saint Peter was where Utrillo and his mother used to eat lunch almost every day; and Adelaide's (where Van Gogh once painted the garden) is where Maurice and Lucie had their reception after the civil ceremony in Paris. Even Adelaide herself is still there, red-headed, bosomy, and with opinions about art. The huge white, immaculate dome of Sacré-Cœur, like the milky nipple of an ample breast, hovers in the background of many vistas, as in so many Utrillo paintings.

And, of course, there is the Lapin Agile, physically unchanged, where Fredé's successor tries to lead the singing in the old way and Wasselet's wax Christ has turned the brown of a mummy from age. The last time I spoke with Utrillo was there in the long-room, the old shooting box of Henri IV. Lucie had allowed him to be driven there, with her and the manservant, so that he could be photographed for a magazine article. The proprietress was deeply honored by his visit and immediately produced a large guest book for him to sign. Instead he asked for drawing materials, and then, seating himself at a table next to the window, looked outside and drew the view. The right foreground of the sketch necessarily consisted of a wall: the wall enclosing the cemetery of Saint Vincent, a very old cemetery that occupies the corner opposite the Lapin Agile. It was the first time in many years that he had composed a Montmartre scene from observation instead of from pictures or memory, and it is reasonable to suppose that it will be the last time.

As I watched him draw, I thought of what Lucie had told me a few days before. The cemetery was filled to its theoretical limit a number of years ago, and thereafter was closed to further interments. Lucie, however, had decided that she and Utrillo should be buried there when they die: "The surroundings have meant so much to him. And a wife should stay with her husband in death as well as in life." She managed to buy a double lot.

I watched his face and his shriveled figure and knew that soon Maurice Utrillo would go back to stay in Montmartre, to the peace that has always eluded him.